STUDENT LABORATORY NOTEBOOK

2nd Edition

Junior Certificate SCIENCE

Published by **MENTOR BOOKS**

All rights reserved

© John Cullen 2009

ISBN: 978-1-906623-28-9

1 3 5 7 9 10 8 6 4 2

Printed in Ireland by Colourbooks Ltd.

STUDENT: _____

SCHOOL: _____

TEACHER: _____

INTRODUCTION

This **Student Laboratory Notebook** allows you to keep a written record or report of the mandatory practical work (Coursework A) that you will carry out as part of the Junior Certificate Science course.

The completed reports on the 30 mandatory activities count for 10% of your final grade in the Junior Certificate examination. It is important therefore, that you take good care of this **Laboratory Notebook**, as neatness and clarity will count when marks are awarded. You will carry out the mandatory activities in small groups (ideally two students per group), however, you should complete your own personal report on each activity, in your own Laboratory Notebook.

The **Student Laboratory Notebook** can be used in conjunction with any of the Junior Certificate Science textbooks currently available. The numbered references next to the title of each activity refer to the possible method described for the activity in **Discovering Science 2nd Edition** (Mentor).

1. You should start each **Activity Report** by putting in the **Date** on which you carried out the activity, in the space provided, next to the **Title**.

2. Complete the **Planning the Activity** section before you carry out the activity.
   This section is very important as it provides evidence that you have planned your approach to the activity and have decided what you should observe and measure in the course of the activity. Completing this section also ensures that you understand the theory behind the activity.

3. The **Materials and Apparatus Used** section should include a list of the equipment that you will use, and an indication of the quantities of chemicals needed.
   Use a pencil to draw a labelled diagram, in the space provided, of the apparatus you used to carry out the activity. Your diagrams should always be clear, neat and well labelled. Simple line drawings, as appear in the Line-Drawings section, at the end of this manual, are ideal, but your diagram should always show the apparatus *you* used to carry out the activity.

4. The **Method** section should include a brief, concise summary, in your own words, of how you carried out the activity. You could mention any special precautions you took.

5. What you observed and/or any result(s) you noted should be included in the **Results** section. A sentence or two is sufficient here.

6. Finally, write your conclusion(s) in the **Conclusion(s)** section. A conclusion is what you can deduce from your observations during the activity or the result(s) you obtained.

Experiments should always be carried out with safety in mind. Make sure that you are familiar with the **Laboratory Safety Rules** given in your textbook, before you start any practical work. Plan your approach to the activity carefully before you start by discussing it with your partner. Make sure that you understand the method you choose to carry out the activity and ask your teacher for advice if you are not sure.

Hopefully, you will enjoy carrying out your practical activities in the laboratory. Science is a practical subject, and, by developing your practical skills in the laboratory, you will increase your understanding and appreciation of science and the scientific method.

Have fun, enjoy your practical work, and best of luck with it!

John Cullen

CONTENTS

Mandatory Investigations and Experiments

Activity   **Page**

1. *Investigate the variety of living things by direct observation of animals and plants in their environment; classify living organisms as plants or animals, and animals as vertebrates or invertebrates*
   - To Investigate the Variety of Living Things *(1.1)* 9

2. *Prepare a slide from plant tissue and sketch the cells under magnification*
   - To Examine Onion Bulb Cells (Plant Cells) *(2.2)* 11

3. *Carry out qualitative food tests for starch, reducing sugar, protein and fat*
   - To Test for the Presence of Starch *(3.2)* 13
   - To Test for the Presence of Glucose, a Reducing Sugar *(3.3)* 14
   - To Test for the Presence of Protein *(3.4)* 15
   - To Test for the Presence of Fats *(3.5)* 15

4. *Investigate the conversion of chemical energy in food to heat energy*
   - To Investigate the Conversion of Chemical Energy in Food to Heat Energy *(3.6)* 16

5. *Investigate the action of amylase on starch; identify substrate, product and enzyme*
   - To Show the Action of Amylase on Starch *(4.1)* 18

6. *Carry out qualitative tests to compare the carbon dioxide levels of inhaled and exhaled air*
   - To Show that Expired Air has More Carbon Dioxide than Inspired Air *(5.1)* 20

7. *Show that starch is produced by a photosynthesising plant*
   - To Show that Starch is Produced in a Photosynthesising Plant *(13.1)* 21

8. *Investigate the conditions necessary for germination*
   - To Investigate the Conditions Needed for Germination *(16.1)* 23

9. *Study a local habitat, using appropriate instruments and simple keys to show the variety and distribution of named organisms*
   - Identification of Plants from the Habitat *(18.2)* 25
   - Collecting and Identifying Animals in the Habitat *(18.3)* 26
   - To Estimate the Numbers of Plants Present in the Habitat *(18.4)* 27

10. *Investigate the presence of micro-organisms in air and soil*
    - To Investigate the Presence of Bacteria and Fungi in Air and Soil *(20.1/20.2)* 28

Activity	Page

11. *To grow crystals using alum or copper sulfate*
- To Grow Crystals of Copper Sulfate *(23.3)* 30

12. *Separate mixtures using a variety of techniques; filtration, evaporation, distillation and paper chromatography*
- To Separate Sand and Water by Filtration *(24.1)* 32
- To Separate Sand, Salt and Water by Filtration and Evaporation *(24.2)* 33
- To Separate Copper Sulfate (or Alcohol) from Water by Distillation *(24.3)* 34
- To Separate the Dyes in Ink by Paper Chromatography *(24.4)* 35

13. *Investigate the pH of a variety of materials using the pH scale*
- To Test the pH of a Variety of Materials Using the pH Scale *(30.1)* 36

14. *Titrate HCl against NaOH, and prepare a sample of NaCl*
- To Titrate Hydrochloric Acid (HCl) Against Sodium Hydroxide (NaOH) and Prepare a Sample of Sodium Chloride (NaCl) *(30.3/30.4)* 38

15. *Show that approximately one fifth of the air is oxygen; show that there is carbon dioxide and water vapour in air*
- To Measure the Percentage of Oxygen in Air *(31.1)* 40
- To Show the Presence of Water Vapour and Carbon Dioxide in Air *(31.2)* 42

16. *Prepare a sample of oxygen by decomposing H_2O_2 using MnO_2 as a catalyst (word equation and chemical equation)*
- To Prepare Oxygen Gas *(31.3)* 44

17. *Prepare carbon dioxide (word and chemical equation), and show that it does not support combustion*
- To Prepare Carbon Dioxide and Show that it Does Not Support Combustion *(31.6)* 46

18. *Conduct a qualitative experiment to detect the presence of dissolved solids in water samples, and test water for hardness (soap test)*
- To Show the Presence of Dissolved Solids in Water Samples *(32.2)* 48
- To Test Various Water Samples for Hardness *(32.4)* 50

19. *Carry out an experiment to demonstrate that oxygen and water are necessary for rusting*
- To Demonstrate that Oxygen and Water are Necessary for Rusting *(34.1)* 52

20. *Investigate the reaction between zinc and HCl, and test for hydrogen (word and chemical equation)*
- To React Zinc with Hydrochloric Acid and Test for Hydrogen *(34.3)* 53

Activity	Page

21. *Identify different forms of energy and carry out simple experiments to show the following energy conversions:*
(a) chemical energy to electrical energy to heat energy,
(b) electrical energy to magnetic energy to kinetic energy,
(c) light energy to electrical energy to kinetic energy

- To Convert Chemical Energy to Electrical Energy to Heat Energy *(37.2)* 55
- To Convert Electrical Energy to Magnetic Energy to Kinetic Energy *(37.3)* 56
- To Convert Light Energy to Electrical Energy to Kinetic Energy *(37.4)* 57

22. *Measure the mass and volume of a variety of solids and liquids and hence determine their densities*

- To Find the Density of a Regularly-Shaped Solid (e.g. a Block of Wood) *(39.1)* 59
- To Find the Density of an Irregularly-Shaped Solid (e.g. a Stone) *(39.2)* 60
- To Find the Density of a Liquid (e.g. Water and Methylated Spirits) *(39.3)* 61

23. *Investigate the relationship between the extension of a spring and the applied force*

- To Investigate the Relationship Between the Extension of a Stretched Spring and the Force Applied to it *(40.1)* 62

24. *Carry out simple experiments to show the transfer of heat energy by conduction, convection and radiation; investigate conduction and convection in water*

- To Compare the Conductivity of Various Metals *(44.1)* 64
- To Show that Water is a Poor Conductor of Heat *(44.2)* 65
- To Show Convection Currents in Water *(44.3)* 66
- To Show Heat Transfer by Radiation *(44.4)* 67

25. *Investigate the expansion of solids, liquids and gases when heated, and contraction when cooled*

- To Show that Solids Expand when Heated and Contract when Cooled *(44.5)* 68
- To Show that Liquids Expand when Heated and Contract when Cooled *(44.6)* 69
- To Show that Gases Expand when Heated and Contract when Cooled *(44.7)* 70

26. *Show that light travels in straight lines and explain how shadows are formed*

- To Show that Light Travels in Straight Lines and Explain how Shadows are Formed *(46.1)* 71

27. *Investigate the reflection of light by plane mirrors, and illustrate this using ray diagrams; demonstrate and explain the operation of a simple periscope*

- To Investigate the Reflection of Light by a Plane Mirror and Show this Using a Ray Diagram *(46.2a)* 72
- To Demonstrate and Explain the Operation of a Simple Periscope *(46.2b)* 73

28. *Plot the magnetic field of a bar magnet*

- To Plot the Magnetic Field of a Bar Magnet *(48.5)* 74

Activity   **Page**

29. *Test electrical conduction in a variety of materials, and classify each material as a conductor or insulator*

- To Distinguish Between Conductors and Insulators *(50.1)* 75

30. *Set up simple electrical circuits; use appropriate instruments to measure current, potential difference (voltage) and resistance, and establish the relationship between them*

- To Set Up a Simple Electrical Circuit and Measure Current, Voltage and Resistance and Show the Relationship Between them *(50.2)* 76

Extra Experiments 78

Line Diagrams for all Mandatory Experiments 80

RECORD OF COMPLETED ACTIVITIES

Mandatory Investigations and Experiments

Activity   **Date Completed**

1. *Investigate the variety of living things by direct observation of animals and plants in their environment; classify living organisms as plants or animals, and animals as vertebrates or invertebrates* ....

2. *Prepare a slide from plant tissue and sketch the cells under magnification* ....

3. *Carry out qualitative food tests for starch, reducing sugar, protein and fat* ....

4. *Investigate the conversion of chemical energy in food to heat energy* ....

5. *Investigate the action of amylase on starch; identify substrate, product and enzyme* ....

6. *Carry out qualitative tests to compare the carbon dioxide levels of inhaled and exhaled air* ....

7. *Show that starch is produced by a photosynthesising plant* ....

8. *Investigate the conditions necessary for germination* ....

9. *Study a local habitat, using appropriate instruments and simple keys to show the variety and distribution of named organisms* ....

10. *Investigate the presence of micro-organisms in air and soil* ....

11. *To grow crystals using alum or copper sulfate* ....

12. *Separate mixtures using a variety of techniques; filtration, evaporation, distillation and paper chromatography* ....

13. *Investigate the pH of a variety of materials using the pH scale* ....

14. *Titrate HCl against NaOH, and prepare a sample of NaCl* ....

15. *Show that approximately one fifth of the air is oxygen; show that there is carbon dioxide and water vapour in air* ....

16. *Prepare a sample of oxygen by decomposing H_2O_2 using MnO_2 as a catalyst (word equation and chemical equation)* ....

Activity	Date Completed
17. Prepare carbon dioxide (word and chemical equation), and show that it does not support combustion	
18. Conduct a qualitative experiment to detect the presence of dissolved solids in water samples, and test water for hardness (soap test)	
19. Carry out an experiment to demonstrate that oxygen and water are necessary for rusting	
20. Investigate the reaction between zinc and HCl, and test for hydrogen (word and chemical equation)	
21. Identify different forms of energy and carry out simple experiments to show the following energy conversions: (a) chemical energy to electrical energy to heat energy, (b) electrical energy to magnetic energy to kinetic energy, (c) light energy to electrical energy to kinetic energy	
22. Measure the mass and volume of a variety of solids and liquids and hence determine their densities	
23. Investigate the relationship between the extension of a spring and the applied force	
24. Carry out simple experiments to show the transfer of heat energy by conduction, convection and radiation; investigate conduction and convection in water	
25. Investigate the expansion of solids, liquids and gases when heated, and contraction when cooled	
26. Show that light travels in straight lines and explain how shadows are formed	
27. Investigate the reflection of light by plane mirrors, and illustrate this using ray diagrams; demonstrate and explain the operation of a simple periscope ..	
28. Plot the magnetic field of a bar magnet	
29. Test electrical conduction in a variety of materials, and classify each material as a conductor or insulator	
30. Set up simple electrical circuits; use appropriate instruments to measure current, potential difference (voltage) and resistance, and establish the relationship between them	

ACTIVITY REPORT   Activity 1   DATE: ....

1. To Investigate the Variety of Living Things *(1.1)*

2. *Planning the Activity:*

(a) What type of area would you chose to visit to see a good variety of living things?
....

(b) Three plants you might expect to find are: .... , ... , ...

(c) Three invertebrates you might find are: .... , ... , ...

(d) Three vertebrates that live in the area are .... , ... , ...

(e) Would you expect to see these vertebrates on the fieldtrip? Explain. ....
....

(f) Name three items or apparatus that might be useful on the fieldtrip (or back in the laboratory) and state why each might be useful.

　1. Item: .... Why useful ....

　2. Item: .... Why useful ....

　3. Item: .... Why useful ....

3. *Materials and Apparatus Used:*
....

4. *Method:* ....
....
....
....
....
....
....
....
....

5. *Results:*

(a) Name 3 plants you identified, and for each, state what feature allowed you to identify it.

　1. Plant: .... Feature: ....

　2. Plant: .... Feature: ....

　3. Plant: .... Feature: ....

(b) Vertebrate animals identified: ....
....

(c) Invertebrate animals identified: ....
....

Draw the animals and plants (a leaf or some other identifying feature) that you identified.
Use a tick to indicate whether each animal is a vertebrate or an invertebrate.

PLANTS IDENTIFIED	ANIMALS IDENTIFIED
1) Name:	1) Name: .... Vertebrate ☐ Invertebrate ☐
2) Name:	2) Name: .... Vertebrate ☐ Invertebrate ☐
3) Name:	3) Name: .... Vertebrate ☐ Invertebrate ☐

6.　*Conclusions:*

....

....

ACTIVITY REPORT   Activity 2   DATE: ....

1. To Examine Onion Bulb Cells (Plant Cells) *(2.2)*

2. *Planning the Activity:*

   (a) Name two instruments that you might use to make things look bigger:

   Instrument 1: .... , Instrument 2: ....

   (b) Light must pass through plant tissue so that you can see the cells using a light microscope. Which part of the onion bulb would be best to use and why?

   ....

   (c) Give the reason for the following steps used to prepare the cells for viewing:

   (i) Placing the plant tissue on a glass slide with a few drops of water, and covering it with a cover-slip:

   ....

   (ii) Using a needle to gently place the cover-slip over the sample:

   ....

   (iii) Using iodine stain on the sample:

   ....

3. *Materials and Apparatus Used:*

   ....

4. *Method Used to Examine the Onion Cells:*

   (a) The mirror or light of the microscope is adjusted so that ....

   ....

   (b) The slide is placed on the centre of the stage to allow ....

   ....

   (c) Looking from the side, the low power objective lens is lowered very close to the slide, and, then looking through the eyepiece, it is slowly raised. Explain why this is done.

   ....

   ....

   ....

   (d) Why is the coarse focus knob never used when viewing cells under medium or high power?

   ....

   (e) How is the iodine stain added to the sample? ....

   ....

   (f) Name 4 parts of the microscope and give the function of each part:

   1) .... Function: ....

   2) .... Function: ....

   3) .... Function: ....

   4) .... Function: ....

5. **Results:**

   Diagrams of Plant Cells (Under Low and High Powers)

   Plant Cells (Low Power):

   Plant Cells (High Power):

6. **Conclusions:**

   ....
   ....
   ....
   ....
   ....

ACTIVITY REPORT   Activity 3   DATE: ....

1. To Test for Starch, Glucose, Protein and Fat *(3.2 - 3.5)*

2. *Planning the Activity:*

You will use various chemicals that will show, by means of a colour change, whether the substance you are testing for (starch, glucose or protein) is present or absent.
What important ability must these chemicals have to be useful in these investigations?

....
....
....
....
....
....
....
....
....

1. To Test for the Presence of Starch *(3.2)*

3. *Materials and Apparatus Used:*

....
....

4. *Method:* ....

....
....
....
....
....
....
....
....
....
....
....

Diagram

5. *Results:* ....

....
....

1. To Test for the Presence of Glucose, a Reducing Sugar *(3.3)*

3. **Materials and Apparatus Used:**
   ....
   ....
   ....

4. **Method:** ....
   ....
   ....
   ....
   ....
   ....
   ....

Diagram

5. **Results:** ....
   ....
   ....

1. To Test for the Presence of Protein *(3.4)*

3. Materials and Apparatus Used:
....
....

4. Method: ....
....
....
....
....
....
....
....

5. Results: ....
....

Diagram

1. To Test for the Presence of Fats *(3.5)*

3. Materials and Apparatus Used:
....
....

4. Method: ....
....
....
....
....

5. Results: ....
....

Diagram

Further Investigations:

Use the food tests you have learned to test each of the following foods for the presence of starch, glucose (or other reducing sugar), protein and fats. Complete the table below:

	Potato	Bread	Pasta	Nut	Soft drink	Egg white	Cooking oil	Cheese	Banana
Starch present?									
Sugar present?									
Protein present?									
Fat present?									

ACTIVITY REPORT   **Activity 4**   DATE: ....

1. **To Investigate the Conversion of Chemical Energy in Food to Heat Energy** *(3.6)*

2. *Planning the Activity:*

    (a) Which food type do you think contains the most energy? ....

    (b) You will be burning different types of food. How will you make sure that it is a fair test?

    ....
    ....
    ....

    (c) State two ways the amount of heat energy in the food could be measured:

    ....
    ....
    ....
    ....

    (d) Which method might be more accurate and why?

    ....
    ....
    ....

3. *Materials and Apparatus Used:*

    ....
    ....
    ....

4. *Method:*

    ....
    ....
    ....
    ....
    ....
    ....
    ....
    ....
    ....
    ....

Diagram

5. *Results:* ....
....
....
....
....
....
....

6. *Conclusions:* ....
....
....
....
....

ACTIVITY REPORT Activity 5 DATE: ....

1. To Show the Action of Amylase on Starch *(4.1)*

2. **Planning the Activity:**

   (a) Name the chemical you would use to test for the presence of starch: ....

   (b) Starch is broken down into sugar by the enzyme called ....

   (c) Sugar is tested for by using .... which turns a ....

   colour when it is .... in a hot water bath at .... °C.

   (d) What would you expect to find in a test tube containing starch and amylase that was then heated in this water bath for five minutes? Explain your answer.

   ....

   ....

3. **Materials and Apparatus Used:** ....

   ....

   ....

   ....

   ....

   ....

Diagram

4. Method:

....
....
....
....
....
....
....
....
....
....

5. Results:

Tube	Containing	Tested with	Results
A	Starch	Iodine	
B	Starch and Amylase	Iodine	
C	Starch and Amylase	Benedict's Solution	

6. Conclusions: ....

....
....
....
....
....
....
....
....
....
....
....

ACTIVITY REPORT Activity 6 DATE: ....

1. **To Show that Expired Air has More Carbon Dioxide than Inspired Air** *(5.1)*

2. *Planning the Activity:*

    (a) Limewater is turned milky in the presence of carbon dioxide. What other feature must limewater have to make it a true test for the presence of carbon dioxide?
    ....

    (b) What type of apparatus would you need to put air containing carbon dioxide through limewater?
    ....

    (c) Why is it better to use a test tube, rather than a beaker or conical flask to hold the limewater?
    ....
    ....

3. *Materials and Apparatus Used:*

    ....

    ....

    ....

    ....

    Diagram

4. *Method:* ....

    ....

    ....

    ....

    ....

    ....

    ....

    ....

    ....

    ....

    ....

5. *Results:*

	Carbon Dioxide Content (High/Low?)	Colour of limewater
Air blown in through **A** (Expired Air)		
Air sucked through **B** (Inspired Air)		

6. *Conclusion:* ....

    ....

ACTIVITY REPORT   Activity 7   DATE: ....

1. To Show that Starch is Produced in a Photosynthesising Plant *(13.1)*

2. *Planning the Activity:*

    (a) What chemical in a leaf shows that it had been photosynthesising? ....

    (b) This chemical is tested for using .... , which turns a .... colour.

    (c) Give two reasons why it would be very difficult to carry out this test on an untreated leaf.

        1) ....

        2) ....

    (d) A leaf from a plant that has been kept in darkness for 48 hours should not contain any

        .... , because the plant has not been able to ....

3. *Materials and Apparatus Used:*

    ....

    ....

4. *Method: (Draw each of the 4 stages of the investigation below)*

A	B
C	D

(a) Why is the leaf dipped in boiling water for one minute (Stage **A**)?

....

....

(b) Why is the leaf placed in hot methylated spirit in the test tube (Stage **B**)?

....

....

(c) Describe the condition of the leaf when it is removed from the methylated spirit:

....

(d) Why does the leaf need to be rinsed in boiling water (Stage **C**)?

....

(e) Describe the method used in Stage **D**

....

....

....

....

(f) Why is the experiment repeated with a leaf from a plant kept in darkness for 48 hours?

....

....

(g) Why should a hot-plate, and not a Bunsen burner be used in this experiment?

....

....

5. **Results:**

....

....

....

....

....

6. **Conclusions:**

....

....

....

....

....

....

ACTIVITY REPORT   Activity 8   DATE: ....

1. To Investigate the Conditions Needed for Germination *(16.1)*

2. *Planning the Activity:*

    (a) Why are cress seeds used for this experiment?
    ....

    (b) Why would you place several seeds in each test tube, and not just one?
    ....

    (c) Why is it necessary to include tube A, which has all the necessary conditions for germination - water, oxygen and heat?
    ....
    ....

    (d) Explain how oxygen is removed from the seeds in tube C?
    ....
    ....

    (e) Heat is removed from test tube D by placing it in a ....

3. *Materials and Apparatus Used:*
    ....
    ....
    ....
    ....

4. *Method:* *The four test tubes are set up as shown below:*

Diagram

....
....
....
....
....
....
....
....

5. *Results:*

Tube	Missing factor (water, oxygen or heat)	Did the seeds germinate?
A		
B		
C		
D		

....
....
....
....

6. *Conclusions:*

....
....
....
....
....

ACTIVITY REPORT   Activity 9   DATE: ....

> **1. To Study a Local Habitat, Using Appropriate Instruments and Simple Keys to Show the Variety and Distribution of Named Organisms** *(18.2 - 18.4)*

2. *Planning the Activity:*

   (a) Name the habitat that you plan to study: ....

   (b) Give two environmental factors that you would measure, and, for each, name the instrument you would need to take the measurements.

      Factor 1) .... Instrument: ....

      Factor 2) .... Instrument: ....

   (c) Three features that a simple map of the habitat should include are:

      1) .... 2) .... 3) ....

   (d) What part of a plant would you usually use to identify it? ....

   (e) What is a quadrat and explain how it is used: ....

      ....

      ....

   (f) Name four pieces of equipment that you will use to collect animals in the habitat:

      1) .... 2) .... 3) .... 4) ....

   (g) How will you identify a plant or animal if you do not recognise it in its habitat?

      ....

      ....

> **1. Identification of Plants from the Habitat** *(18.2)*

3. *Materials Used:* ....

4. *Method:* ....

   ....

   ....

5. *Results:* (sketch a leaf of each of three plants you identified using a key).

Plant Name:	Plant Name:	Plant Name: ....

1. Collecting and Identifying Animals in the Habitat *(18.3)*

3. **Equipment Used:**
   ....

4. **Method:** *(sketch four different methods used to collect animals).*

Method:	Method: ....
Method:	Method: ....

5. **Results:** *(Name 5 animals you found, and give 2 features of each that helped you identify them).*

   1) .... Feature 1) .... Feature 2) ....

   2) .... Feature 1) .... Feature 2) ....

   3) .... Feature 1) .... Feature 2) ....

   4) .... Feature 1) .... Feature 2) ....

   5) .... Feature 1) .... Feature 2) ....

6. **Conclusions:** *(comment on the usefulness of each of the collection methods you used).*

   Method: .... ; ....

   Method: .... ; ....

   Method: .... ; ....

   Method: .... ; ....

1. To Estimate the Numbers of Plants Present in the Habitat *(18.4)*

3. *Equipment Used:* ....

4. *Method:* ....
   ....
   ....
   ....
   ....

5. *Results:*

Plant Name	Quadrat Number										Total (%)
	1	2	3	4	5	6	7	8	9	10	
1)											
2)											
3)											
4)											
5)											
6)											

Present your results in a bar chart below:

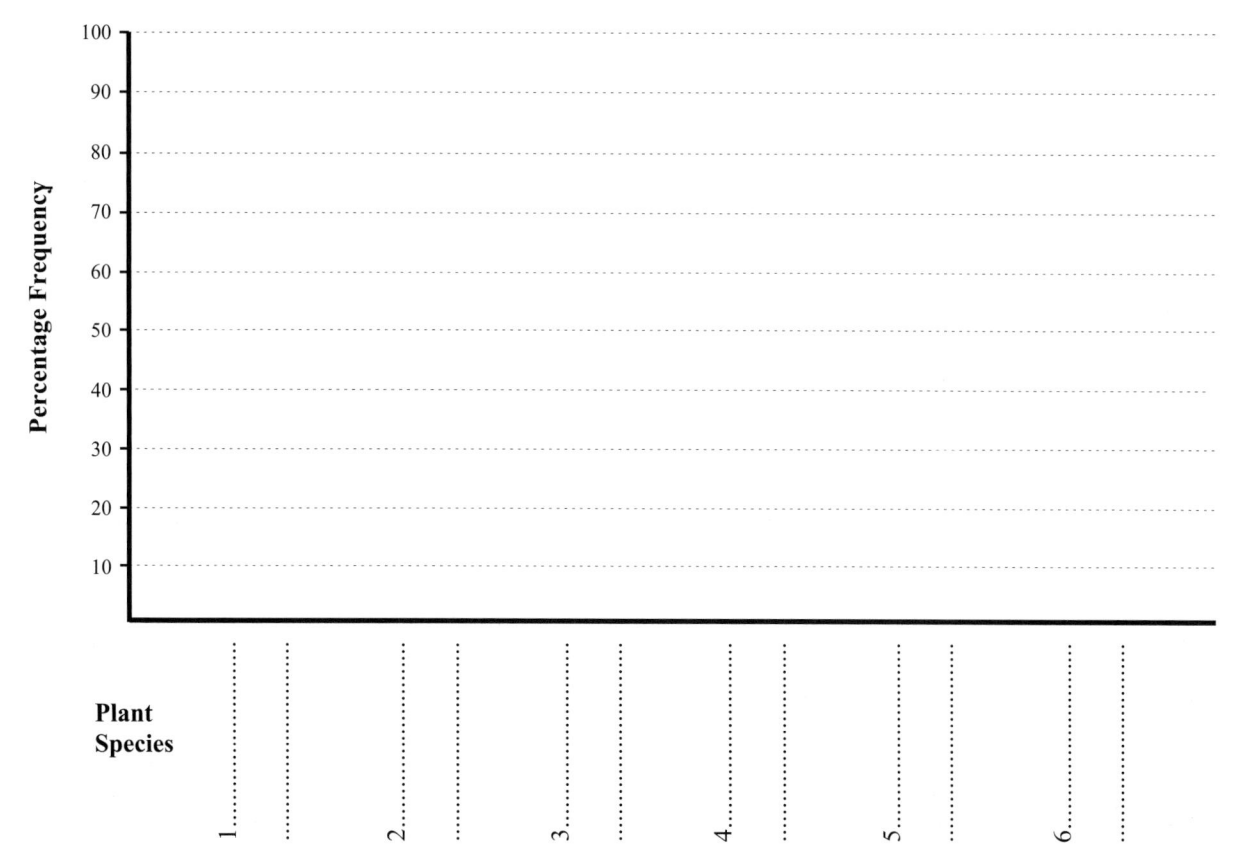

[Bar chart with y-axis "Percentage Frequency" (0–100) and x-axis "Plant Species" (1–6)]

ACTIVITY REPORT   **Activity 10**   DATE: ....

1. **To Investigate the Presence of Bacteria and Fungi in Air and Soil** *(20.1/20.2)*

2. *Planning the Activity:*

   (a) Micro-organisms grow successfully when they have nutrients, moisture and warmth. How would you provide each of these requirements during this investigation?

      1) Nutrients: ....

      2) Moisture: ....

      3) Warmth: ....

   (b) What is the purpose of growing micro-organisms in this investigation?

      ....

      ....

   (c) Why must the agar and petri dishes be sterilised before the investigation?

      ....

   (d) Why would you leave one of the petri dishes unopened during the investigation?

      ....

   (e) Why is sterilised soil placed on one of the agar petri dishes?

      ....

   (f) How would you sterilise a soil sample?

      ....

   (g) Why is the incubator (oven) kept at 20ºC and not at a higher temperature?

      ....

   (h) Why are the petri dishes placed upside-down in the incubator?

      ....

   (i) Why would you tape the petri dishes shut before examining the results?

      ....

3. *Materials and Apparatus Used:* ....

....

....

4. *Method:* ....

....

....

....

....

....
....
....
....
....
....

5. Results: *(Draw the results for each of the four agar plates below).*

1) *exposed to air*

2) *unopened*

3) *fresh soil*

4) *sterile soil*

6. Conclusions: ....
....
....
....
....
....

ACTIVITY REPORT.   Activity 11   DATE: ....

1. **To Grow Crystals of Copper Sulfate** *(23.3)*

2. *Planning the Activity:*

   (a) How would you make a hot, concentrated solution of copper sulfate?

   ....

   ....

   ....

   ....

   (b) When this solution is allowed to cool, what would you expect to see in the test tube?

   ....

3. *Materials and Apparatus Used:* ....

   ....

4. *Method:*

   Diagram

   ....

   ....

   ....

5. *Results:* ....

   (a) Small crystals are formed when: ....

   (b) Large crystals are formed when: ....

   (c) The solution that remains above the crystals is called a .... solution

   because it cannot .... at that temperature.

6. *Conclusions:* ....

   ....

ACTIVITY REPORT   Activity 12   DATE: ....

1. **To Separate Mixtures by (1) Filtration; (2) Evaporation; (3) Distillation; and, (4) Paper Chromatography** *(24.1 - 24.4)*

2. *Planning the Activity:*

(a) Substances in a mixture can be separated if they have a difference in their physical properties. For each of the following mixtures, give a physical difference that allows them to be separated.

1) sand and water: ....
....

2) salt and water: ....
....

3) alcohol and water: ....
....

4) different dyes in black ink: ....
....

(b) How does a tea bag work to keep the tea leaves in but allow the tea out into the pot?
....

(c) How might this principle be used to separate sand from water?
....

(d) On a sunny day, what happens to a puddle of water caused by a shower of rain?
....

(e) What would happen to any substances that were dissolved in the puddle of water?
....

(f) If a mixture of alcohol and water was gently heated, which part of the mixture would evaporate first and why?
....

(g) What would cause a liquid that has evaporated, and is now a gas, to turn back into a liquid again?
....

(h) Using your reasoning in (f) and (g), describe how a distillery would make brandy (mainly alcohol) from wine (a mixture of water and alcohol).
....

(i) If ten people in your class ran a 5 km race, they would probably end up being separated out. What is the reason for this?
....

(j) Some of the coloured dyes in black ink are more soluble than others. How might this physical difference be used to separate them out?
....
....

1. To Separate Sand and Water by Filtration *(24.1)*

3. **Materials and Apparatus Used:**

   ....
   ....
   ....

4. **Method:** ....

   ....
   ....
   ....
   ....
   ....
   ....

Diagram

5. **Result:** ....

   ....
   ....

1. To Separate Sand, Salt and Water by Filtration and Evaporation *(24.2)*

3. **Materials and Apparatus Used:**

....

....

....

4. **Method:** ....

....

....

....

....

....

....

Diagram

5. **Result:** ....

....

....

1. To Separate Copper Sulfate (or Alcohol) from Water by Distillation *(24.3)*

3. Materials and Apparatus Used:

....
....
....

4. Method: ....

....
....
....
....
....

Diagram

5. Result: ....

....
....

1. **To Separate the Dyes in Ink by Paper Chromatography** *(24.4)*

3. *Materials and Apparatus Used:*

   ....

   ....

   ....

4. *Method:* ....

   ....

   ....

   ....

   ....

   ....

   ....

Diagram

5. *Result:* ....

   ....

   ....

ACTIVITY REPORT — Activity 13 — DATE: ....

1. To Test the pH of a Variety of Materials Using the pH Scale *(30.1)*

2. **Planning the Activity:**

   (a) Name five different substances that you could use that you think *might* be acids:

   1) .... , 2) .... , 3) .... , 4) .... , 5) ....

   (b) Name five different substances that you could use that you think *might* be bases:

   1) .... , 2) .... , 3) .... , 4) .... , 5) ....

   (c) How would you plan an experiment to test if each of the substances you named in (a) and (b) is an acid or a base?

   ....

   ....

   ....

   ....

   (d) How would you alter the experiment to find out *how* acidic or *how* basic the substance being tested is?

   ....

   (e) How would you ensure that the method you choose is a 'fair test'?

   ....

   ....

   (f) The pH scale is used to measure how acidic or how alkaline a solution is.

   A solution whose pH is less than 7 is said to be ....

   A solution whose pH is 7 is said to be ....

   A solution whose pH is greater than 7 is said to be ....

   (g) The colour of .... paper changes in solutions of different pH.

   (h) Soaps that are neither acidic nor alkaline are considered to be better for the skin.
   Describe how you would carry out a *fair test* on two brands of soap to find out which of them might be better for the skin.

   ....

   ....

   ....

   ....

   ....

3. **Materials and Apparatus Used:** ....

   ....

   ....

4. Method:

Diagram

....
....
....
....

5. Results:

Substance Tested	Colour Observed	pH
1)		
2)		
3)		
4)		
5)		
6)		
7)		
8)		
9)		
10)		

6. Conclusions: ....

....

ACTIVITY REPORT   Activity 14   DATE: ....

1. To Titrate Hydrochloric Acid (HCl) Against Sodium Hydroxide (NaOH) and Prepare a Sample of Sodium Chloride (NaCl) *(30.3, 30.4)*

2. Planning the Activity:

(a) An acid and a base neutralise each other to give a .... and ....

(b) Hydrochloric acid (formula ....) neutralises sodium hydroxide (formula ....) to form the salt, sodium chloride (formula ....) and water (formula ....).

(c) The chemical equation for this reaction is:

.... + ... $\longrightarrow$ .... + ...

(d) A titration experiment aims to discover what exact volume of an acid is needed to just neutralise a certain volume of an alkali (i.e. a base in solution).
How would you show that a colourless liquid in a conical flask is a solution of a base (an alkali)?

....

(e) If you were now to slowly add acid to the conical flask, what would you expect to observe?

....

....

(f) How would you know when you had added just enough acid to neutralise the base?

....

(g) What three substances would then be present in the conical flask?
1) .... , 2) .... , 3) ....

(h) Why is it important that the volumes of the alkali and acid used are measured very carefully?

....

....

(i) Knowing these volumes, the titration could then be repeated, but without using any ....
....

(j) In this final titration, what two substances should be present in the conical flask at the end?
1) .... , 2) ....

(k) How might you go about seeing the dissolved compound which should now be present in the conical flask?

....

....

....

....

....

(l) What two quantities would you need to measure during the course of this experiment?

1) ....

2) ....

3. **Materials and Apparatus Used:** ....

....

Diagram

4. **Method:** ....

....

....

....

....

....

....

5. **Results:**

Titration Number	1	2	Average value
Volume of acid added			

6. **Conclusions:** ....

....

ACTIVITY REPORT   Activity 15   DATE: ....

To Measure the Percentage of Oxygen in Air and Show that there is Carbon Dioxide and Water Vapour in Air *(31.1, 31.2)*

1. To Measure the Percentage of Oxygen in Air *(31.1)*

2. *Planning the Activity:*

    (a) When something burns in air, it uses the .... in the air to form a compound called an ....

    (b) The effect of this is to remove the .... from the air.

    (c) If the burning is done inside a closed container, then the volume of air missing at the end, equals the volume of .... that was in the air.

3. *Materials and Apparatus Used:* ....

    ....

    ....

    ....

    ....

    ....

    ....

Diagram

4. **Method:** ....
....
....
....
....
....
....
....
....
....
....
....

What changes occurred in the copper metal? Explain. ....
....
....
....

5. **Results:**

Volume of air in the syringe at the start:	=	.... cm^3
Volume of gas in the syringe at the end:	=	.... cm^3
Volume of oxygen used up in burning:	=	.... cm^3
Percentage of oxygen in air:	=	.... %

6. **Conclusion:** ....
....
....
....

1. To Show the Presence of Water Vapour and Carbon Dioxide in Air *(31.2)*

2. *Planning the Activity:*

   (a) On a cold winter's day, what might you notice on the inside of the window pane? ....

   (b) This liquid came from the .... and formed by the process of ....
       on the window pane, which provided a .... surface, allowing this to happen.

   (c) You could not be sure that this liquid was water, it would need to be tested using a piece of
       .... paper, which would change colour from .... to ....
       if water was present.

   (d) Carbon dioxide is tested for by passing it through .... which turns a
       .... colour if carbon dioxide is present.

   (e) Air you would breathe out would quickly affect the colour of limewater. Explain why this is so.
       ....

   (f) What method would you use to pass air from the room through the limewater?
       ....

   (g) Why should limewater be stored in a sealed container?
       ....

3. *Materials and Apparatus Used:* ....
   ....
   ....

Diagram

4. *Method:*

   ....
   ....
   ....
   ....
   ....
   ....
   ....
   ....
   ....
   ....

   (a) Air is taken into each test tube in the .... tubes and out in the .... tubes.

   (b) Ice and water are placed in the beaker so that: ....
   ....

   (c) Cobalt chloride paper must be dried before it is used so that its colour is .... , it then changes colour to .... in the presence of water.

5. *Results:*

   ....
   ....
   ....
   ....

6. *Conclusions:*

   ....
   ....
   ....
   ....

ACTIVITY REPORT   Activity 16   DATE: ....

1. *To Prepare Oxygen Gas* (31.3)

2. *Planning the Activity:*

(a) Hydrogen peroxide (formula H_2O_2) can be broken down into .... (formula ....) and .... (formula ....).

(b) The chemical .... (formula ....) speeds up this reaction. A chemical that is used to speed up a reaction is called a ....

(c) Explain why mixing the two chemicals in a beaker or test tube would not be a suitable method for carrying out this experiment: ....
....
....

(d) Describe how the oxygen produced might be collected: ....
....
....

(e) How would you fill a gas jar with water and then turn it upside-down without the water spilling out?
....
....

(f) Why should the basin (or trough) not be filled to the very brim with water at the start of the experiment? ....

(g) Why should the first gas jar full of gas be discarded? ....
....

(h) What precaution is needed when placing the gas jar cover on the gas jar?
....
....

(i) Give two reasons why a tap funnel and not an ordinary funnel is used in this experiment:
  1) ....
  2) ....

(j) Hydrogen peroxide is a dangerous chemical that can cause burns. Give two safety precautions needed when using it.
  1) ....
  2) ....

3. *Materials and Apparatus Used:* ....
....
....
....

4. **Method:**

Diagram

Say where the chemicals are placed ....

....

....

How is the gas jar set up to collect the gas? ....

....

....

Describe the procedure ....

....

....

....

5. **Results:** ....

....

6. **Conclusions:** ....

....

ACTIVITY REPORT   Activity 17   DATE: ....

1. To Prepare Carbon Dioxide and Show it Does Not Support Combustion *(31.6)*

2. *Planning the Activity:*

(a) Carbon dioxide is prepared by reacting an acid with a carbonate.

The acid used is .... acid (formula ....) and the carbonate used is ....

carbonate, also known as .... chips.

(b) Carbon dioxide is a colourless, odourless, tasteless gas. How would you know if you had collected

it? ....

(c) The word equation for the preparation of carbon dioxide is:

.... + ... ⟶

.... + ... + ...

(d) The chemical equation for the preparation of carbon dioxide is:

.... + ... ⟶ .... + ... + ...

(e) Where will the salt, calcium chloride, be deposited during the preparation of carbon dioxide?

....

(f) What problem might this cause during the preparation?

....

....

(g) How would you get around this problem?

....

....

(h) Why should the tap of the tap funnel be kept closed when all the hydrochloric acid has been

passed through? ....

....

(i) Dilute hydrochloric acid can irritate your skin; give two safety precautions required when using it.

1) ....

2) ....

(j) How would you show that carbon dioxide does not support combustion (burning)?

....

....

3. *Materials and Apparatus Used:* ....

....

....

4. Method:

Diagram

Say where the chemicals are placed..
....
....

How is the gas jar set up to collect the gas? ....
....
....

Describe the procedure ....
....

Testing for combustion ....
....

5. Results: ....
....
....

6. Conclusions: ....
....

ACTIVITY REPORT   Activity 18   DATE: ....

To Show the Presence of Dissolved Solids in Water Samples and To Test Water Samples for Hardness *(32.2, 32.4)*

1. To Show the Presence of Dissolved Solids in Water Samples *(32.2)*

2. *Planning the Activity:*

(a) Why, do you think, would tap water, river water, mineral water etc. contain dissolved solids?

....

(b) Would you expect rainwater to contain dissolved solids? Explain. ....

....

(c) From your experiments on separating mixtures, can you suggest a method in the laboratory that would allow you to see the dissolved solids?

....

....

3. *Materials and Apparatus Used:*

....

....

....

Diagram

4. Method: ....

....

....

....

....

....

....

....

....

5. Results:

Water Sample Tested	Amount of Dissolved Solids
1)	
2)	
3)	
4)	
5)	
6)	
7)	
8)	

....

....

....

....

....

6. Conclusions: ....

....

....

....

....

....

1. To Test Various Water Samples for Hardness *(32.4)*

2. Planning the Activity:

(a) What causes hardness in water? ....

(b) How would you investigate whether a sample was hard water or soft water?

....

....

(c) How might you modify this investigation to find out how much hardness was in a water sample?

....

(d) What measurements would you take to discover how hard various water samples were?

....

3. Materials and Apparatus Used:

....

....

....

....

....

....

Diagram

4. *Method:*

...

5. *Results:*

Name of Water Sample (1 - 6)	1)	2)
Number of Drops of Soap Solution		

3)	4)	5)	6)

...

6. *Conclusions:* ...

ACTIVITY REPORT   Activity 19   DATE: ....

1. To Demonstrate that Oxygen and Water are Necessary for Rusting *(34.1)*

2. *Planning the Activity:*

   (a) You are given some iron nails and any equipment and chemicals you might need; how could you arrange it so that one nail has no oxygen available to it?

   ....

   (b) How might you arrange it so that another nail has no water (even water vapour in the air) available to it?

   ....

   (c) At the end of one week, if the nails had not rusted, someone might say, 'Well, they wouldn't have rusted in that short a time anyway - it has nothing to do with them having no oxygen or water!'. What would you need to include in your experiment to answer this person?

   ....

   ....

3. *Materials and Apparatus Used:* ....

   ....

Diagram

4. *Method:* ....

   ....

   ....

   ....

5. *Results:* ....

   ....

6. *Conclusion:* ....

ACTIVITY REPORT   Activity 20   DATE: ....

1. To React Zinc with Hydrochloric Acid and Test for Hydrogen *(34.3)*

2. *Planning the Activity:*

(a) Hydrogen is prepared by reacting an acid with a metal.

The acid used is .... acid (formula ....) and the metal used is ....

(b) The word equation for this preparation of hydrogen is:

.... + ... metal ⟶

.... + ...

(c) Why will you not be able to see the compound formed in this reaction?

....

(d) The chemical equation for the preparation of hydrogen is:

.... + ... ⟶ .... + ...

(e) Why would you not use calcium or magnesium as the metal in this experiment?

....

(f) Why would you collect the hydrogen gas in test tubes rather than in gas jars?

....

(g) Why is the test tube full of hydrogen stoppered under water? ....

....

(h) Hydrogen is a colourless, odourless, tasteless gas. How would you know if you had collected it? ....

(i) Suppose you were supplied with the following items in the laboratory:
Test tube, single holed stopper, glass tubing, rubber tubing, glass funnel, beaker, wax taper, dilute hydrochloric acid, zinc metal, and childrens' 'bubble liquid'.

Describe how you could use these items to show two important properties of hydrogen.

....

....

....

....

....

....

....

....

(j) What two properties of hydrogen could you show with this experiment that you have designed?

1) ....

2) ....

(k) Why is hydrogen not found in the mixture of gases that make up air?

....

3. **Materials and Apparatus Used:** ....
   ....
   ....

Diagram

---

4. **Method:** *Setting up the experiment:*..
   ....
   ....

   Testing for hydrogen: ....
   ....

5. **Results:** *(What do you observe?):* ....
   ....
   ....

   What was the result of the test for hydrogen?: ....
   ....

6. **Conclusion:** ....
   ....

ACTIVITY REPORT   Activity 21   DATE: ....

To Investigate Energy Conversions *(37.2 - 37.4)*

1. To Convert Chemical Energy to Electrical Energy to Heat Energy *(37.2)*

2. *Planning the Activity:*

    (a) A battery is used to convert .... energy into .... energy.

    (b) An electric bulb can convert .... energy into .... and .... energy.

    (c) How would you know that these energy conversions had taken place in the bulb?

    ....

3. *Materials Used:* ....

    ....

Diagram

4. *Method:* ....

    ....

    ....

5. *Results:* ....

    ....

    ....

6. *Conclusions:* The experiment shows that chemical energy in the .... is converted to electrical energy in the .... and then to .... and .... energy in the ....

1. To Convert Electrical Energy to Magnetic Energy to Kinetic Energy *(37.3)*

2. ***Planning the Activity:***

    (a) A wire, with an electric current flowing through it has a .... around it.

    (b) When the wire is wrapped around an iron .... , the .... becomes a .... , in other words, it gains .... energy.

    (c) Electrical energy from the battery or power pack is converted to .... energy in the iron nail, which is converted to .... energy in the paper clips.

    (d) What happens to the paper clips when the current is switched off? Explain.

    ....

3. ***Materials Used:*** ....

    ....

    Diagram

4. ***Method:*** ....

    ....

    ....

5. ***Results:*** ....

    ....

6. ***Conclusions:*** The experiment shows that electrical energy in the .... is converted to magnetic energy in the .... and then to kinetic energy in the ....

1. To Convert Light Energy to Electrical Energy to Kinetic Energy *(37.4)*

2. *Planning the Activity:*

    (a) A solar panel converts .... energy to .... energy if it is placed in strong sunlight, or if a bright light is shone on it.

    (b) The .... energy in the wires is converted into .... energy in the needle of a galvanometer, or in a tiny motor.

    (c) How would you increase the amount of light energy received by the solar cell?
    ....

    (d) If the light energy was increased what effect would you expect this to have on the kinetic energy?
    ....

    (e) How would you test to see if your theory in (d) is correct?
    ....

3. *Materials Used:* ....
   ....

Diagram

4. *Method:* ....
   ....
   ....

5. *Results:* ....

6. *Conclusions:* The experiment shows that the solar panel converts .... energy to .... energy and the .... energy is converted to .... energy in the galvanometer.

ACTIVITY REPORT   Activity 22   DATE: ....

> *1.* **To Determine the Densities of Solids and Liquids** *(39.1 - 39.3)*

2. *Planning the Activity:*

(a) The density of a substance is the mass per unit volume of it.
Therefore, to find the density of a substance, you must measure two things - the .... of it, measured in .... , and the .... of it, measured in ....

(b) The .... is then divided by the .... to find the density, measured in ....

(c) The mass of an object is found by using an ....

(d) How would you find the volume of a rectangular block of wood?
....

(e) What two pieces of equipment would you use to measure the volume of an irregularly-shaped object (e.g. a stone)?
1) .... , 2) ....

(f) Describe how you might measure the volume of a stone.
....
....
....

(g) If the irregularly-shaped object floats in water, how would you then measure its volume?
....
....

(h) Why is it important that you would find the mass of the stone *before* finding its volume?
....
....

(i) What *three* measurements would you have to take to find the mass of a liquid?
1) ....
2) ....
3) ....

(j) Give two precautions you should take when measuring the volume of a liquid in a graduated cylinder:
1) ....
2) ....

(k) An object will sink in water if its density is greater than the .... of .... which is .... g/cm^3.

(l) Why do you think, a ship made of steel, of density 7.9 g/cm^3 floats on water?
....
....
....

1. To Find the Density of a Regularly-Shaped Solid (e.g. a Block of Wood) *(39.1)*

3. *Materials and Apparatus Used:* ....

   ....

Diagram

4. *Method: To measure the volume of the block:*..

   ....

   To measure the mass of the block: ....

   ....

   ....

5. *Results:*

Material of Block Used	Mass of Block (g)	Length (cm)	Width (cm)	Height (cm)	Volume (cm^3)	Density (g/cm^3)
1)						
2)						
3)						

6. *Conclusion:* ....

1. To Find the Density of an Irregularly-Shaped Solid (e.g. a Stone) *(39.2)*

3. *Materials and Apparatus Used:* ....
   ....
   ....

Diagram

4. *Method:* To measure the volume of the stone: ....
   ....
   ....
   ....
   ....

   To measure the mass of the stone: ....

5. *Results:*

Stone	Mass of Stone (g)	Volume (cm^3)	Density (g/cm^3)
1)			
2)			
3)			

6. *Conclusion:* ....
   ....

1. To Find the Density of a Liquid (e.g. Water and Methylated Spirits) *(39.3)*

3. *Materials and Apparatus Used:* ....
   ....
   ....

Diagram

4. *Method: To measure the volume of the liquid:* ....
   ....

   To measure the mass of the liquid: ....
   ....
   ....

5. *Results:*

Liquid	Volume of Liquid (cm³)	Mass of Empty Beaker (g)	Mass of Beaker + Liquid (g)	Mass of Liquid (g)	Density of Liquid (g/cm³)
1)					
2)					
3)					

6. *Conclusion:* ....
   ....

ACTIVITY REPORT	Activity 23	DATE: ....

1. To Investigate the Relationship Between the Extension of a Spiral Spring and the Force Applied to it *(40.1)*

2. *Planning the Activity:*

   (a) If you fixed one end of a spiral spring to a retort stand, and attached a weight to the other end, what, do you think, would happen to the spring?

   ....

   (b) What would happen if you attached a weight that was twice as heavy as the first weight?

   ....

   (c) What would happen if you attached a weight that was three times as heavy as the first weight?

   ....

   (d) What is the relationship between the size of the weight attached (i.e. the force applied) and what you might observe to happen to the spring?

   ....

   ....

3. *Materials and Apparatus Used:*

   Diagram

   ....

   ....

   ....

   ....

4. *Method:*

   ....

   ....

   ....

   ....

   ....

   ....

   ....

   ....

   ....

   ....

5. *Results:*

Force (weight) in Newtons	0							
Extension of Spring (in cm's)	0							

5. Results: *(Present your results as a graph, putting Force (in newtons) on the horizontal axis)*

6. Conclusion:

(a) How would you describe the graph you have drawn? ....

....

(b) Where have you seen a graph like this before? ....

....

(c) What does a graph like this tell you about the relationship between the extension of the spring and the force applied to it?

....

....

....

(d) Describe how you could use the equipment and the graph to find the weight of your pencil case.

....

....

....

ACTIVITY REPORT   Activity 24   DATE: ....

To Show the Transfer of Heat Energy by Conduction, Convection and Radiation; to Investigate Conduction and Convection in Water *(44.1 - 44.4)*

1. **To Compare the Conductivity of Various Metals** *(44.1)*

2. *Planning the Activity:*

   (a) Describe what would happen if one end of a solid rod was heated: ....
   ....

   (b) How would you show that this had happened? ....
   ....

   (c) Give three precautions you would take to carry out a fair test to see whether copper or glass was a better conductor of heat.

   1) ....

   2) ....

   3) ....

3. *Materials Used:* ....
   ....

   Diagram

4. *Method:* ....
   ....
   ....

5. *Results:* ....
   ....

6. *Conclusion:* ....

1. To Show that Water is a Poor Conductor of Heat *(44.2)*

2. *Planning the Activity:*

    (a) The water at the *bottom* of a test tube that is being heated near the *top* is heated by conduction and not by convection. How do you know that this must be so?

    ....

    (b) Why would you need to add a weight to the test tube? ....

    (c) If the water at the top of the test tube was made to boil, what would you expect to happen to the ice at the bottom of the test tube?

    ....

    (d) A dual immersion heater has two heating elements, one near the top and one at the bottom. Why is this arrangement suitable for either heating (i) just enough water for the hand basin, or, (ii) enough water to have a bath?

    (i) ....

    (ii) ....

3. *Materials Used:* ....

    ....

Diagram

4. *Method:* ....

    ....

5. *Results:* ....

    ....

6. *Conclusions:*   Water is a very poor .... of ....

1. To Show Convection Currents in Water *(44.3)*

2. Planning the Activity:

(a) When a liquid is heated it .... and therefore becomes less ....

The heated liquid will then .... in the beaker and be replaced by ....

liquid from the top of the beaker. This movement of the liquid is called a ....

current. It occurs in liquids and .... , the molecules of which can ....

(b) What needs to be added to the beaker of liquid to allow you to see the convection current?

....

(c) Why, do you think, should the element of an electric kettle be placed as close to the bottom of the kettle as possible?

....

....

3. Materials Used: ....

....

Diagram

4. Method: ....

....

....

....

5. Results: ....

6. Conclusions: ....

....

1. To Show Heat Transfer by Radiation *(44.4)*

2. ***Planning the Activity:***

    (a) A can filled with boiling water loses heat by conduction, convection and radiation. Explain how it loses heat by each of these methods.

    1) Conduction: ....

    2) Convection: ....

    3) Radiation: ....

    (b) Why is the thermometer placed beside the can and not above it?

    ....

    ....

    (c) What effect would painting the silver can a matt black colour have on the results of the experiment?

    ....

3. ***Materials Used:*** ....

    ....

Diagram

4. ***Method:*** ....

    ....

    ....

    ....

5. ***Result:*** ....

6. ***Conclusions:*** ....

    ....

ACTIVITY REPORT   Activity 25   DATE: ....

To Investigate the Expansion of Solids, Liquids and Gases when Heated, and Contraction when Cooled *(44.5 - 44.7)*

1. **To Show that Solids Expand when Heated and Contract when Cooled** *(44.5)*

2. *Planning the Activity:*

   (a) You are given a metal ball and a ring that it just fits through. If the ball expanded after heating it, how would you show that it had expanded?

   ....

   (b) Why are there gaps left between railway tracks as they are being laid?

   ....

   (c) Why are electric cables left with some slack as they are hung from pole to pole?

   ....

3. *Materials Used:* ....

   Diagram

4. *Method:* ....

   ....

   ....

5. *Results:* ....

   ....

6. *Conclusions:* ....

   ....

   ....

1. To Show that Liquids Expand when Heated and Contract when Cooled *(44.6)*

2. *Planning the Activity:*

    (a) Why would you use a long, glass tube in this experiment?
    ....

    (b) Why would you colour the water with food dye or potassium permanganate crystals?
    ....

    (c) If the heated water in the flask was allowed to cool, what would you observe to happen?
    ....

    (d) Give one practical use for the way a liquid behaves when heated or cooled
    ....

3. *Materials Used:* ....
    ....

Diagram

4. *Method:* ....
    ....
    ....

5. *Results:* ....
    ....

6. *Conclusions:* ....
    ....

1. To Show that Gases Expand when Heated and Contract when Cooled *(44.7)*

2. **Planning the Activity:**

   (a) What gas is being heated and cooled in this experiment? ....

   (b) Why do bubbles appear in the water in the beaker? ....
   ....

   (c) What do you think would happen when the flask is allowed to cool. Why would this happen?
   ....

3. **Materials Used:** ....
   ....
   ....

Diagram

4. **Method:** ....
   ....
   ....
   ....

5. **Results:** ....
   ....
   ....

6. **Conclusions:** ....
   ....

ACTIVITY REPORT   Activity 26   DATE: ....

1. **To Show that Light Travels in Straight Lines and Explain how Shadows are Formed** *(46.1)*

2. Planning the Activity:

(a) How do you know that light reaching your eye from an object, has travelled in straight lines?

....

(b) A shadow is an area of darkness directly behind an object lit from the front. What information do shadows give about the way light travels?

....

(c) How would you ensure that the three holes in the cards are in a straight line?

....

3. Materials Used: ....

....

Diagram

4. Method: ....

....

....

5. Results: ....

....

6. Conclusion: ....

....

Shadows are formed due to the fact that ....

71

ACTIVITY REPORT Activity 27 DATE: ....

To Investigate the Reflection of Light by Plane Mirrors and Show this Using a Ray Diagram and to Demonstrate the Operation of a Simple Periscope *(46.2)*

1. **To Investigate the Reflection of Light by a Plane Mirror and Draw a Ray Diagram** *(46.2a)*

2. *Planning the Activity:*

    (a) How would you produce a single light ray using a ray box?

    ....

    (b) Why would you carry out this experiment in a darkened room?

    ....

    (c) How would you measure the angle the entering light ray makes to the normal, and the angle the exiting light ray makes to the normal? What is always the relationship between these two angles?

    ....

    ....

3. *Materials Used:* ....

    Ray Diagram

4. *Method:* ....

    ....

5. *Results:* ....

    ....

6. *Conclusion:* ....

    The entering (incident) ray always makes an angle to the normal .... to the angle made by the exiting (reflected) ray to the normal.

1. To Demonstrate and Explain the Operation of a Simple Periscope *(46.2b)*

2. **Planning the Activity:**

   (a) Crouch down behind your desk and hold two plane mirrors, one in each hand, in such a way that you can now see over the top of the desk.

   (b) Given a long, rectangular cardboard box, measuring 50 cm by 8 cm by 8 cm, two plane mirrors, 'Blu-tack' and a pair of scissors, describe how you would make a simple periscope.

   ....

   ....

   ....

   ....

   (c) What angle should the mirrors be to the horizontal? Why is this important?

   ....

3. **Materials Used:** ....

   ....

   ....

   ....

   ....

   Diagram

4. **Method:**

   ....

   ....

   ....

   ....

   ....

   ....

   ....

   ....

   ....

   ....

   ....

   ....

   ....

5. **Results:** ....

   ....

6. **Conclusion:** ....

   A periscope can be used to: ....

ACTIVITY REPORT   Activity 28   DATE: ....

1. To Plot the Magnetic Field of a Bar Magnet *(48.5)*

2. *Planning the Activity:*

    (a) You will use (i) iron filings, and (ii) plotting compasses to investigate the magnetic field of a bar magnet. What information would each of these give about the magnetic field?

    (i) iron filings: ....

    (ii) plotting compasses: ....

    (b) Why would you place a sheet of paper over the magnet when using iron filings?

    ....

    (c) Why does the needle of a plotting compass always points towards the south pole of the bar magnet?

    ....

    ....

3. *Materials Used:* ....

4. *Method:*

    Diagram

    [S   N]

    ....

    ....

5. *Results:* ....

    ....

    ....

6. *Conclusion:* ....

    The magnetic field around a bar magnet can be plotted using .... and ....

    The magnetic field lines run from the .... pole to the .... pole of the bar magnet.

ACTIVITY REPORT   Activity 29   DATE: ....

1. To Distinguish Between Conductors and Insulators *(50.1)*

2. *Planning the Activity:*

   (a) You will use a simple electric circuit to test various substances to see if they are good conductors or insulators of electricity. Name four items each that you think might be made of a substance that is (i) a conductor, and (ii) an insulator.

   (i) possible conductors: ....

   (ii) possible insulators: ....

   (b) Given a battery, a bulb, wires and two crocodile clips, describe how you would go about setting up a circuit that could be used to test for conductors or insulators

   ....

   ....

3. *Materials Used:* ....

   ....

   Diagram

4. *Method:* ....

   ....

5. *Results:* good conductors include: ....

   ....

   good insulators include: ....

   ....

6. *Conclusion: in general,* .... *are good conductors of electricity, and* ....-........................ *are good insulators of electricity.*

ACTIVITY REPORT   Activity 30   DATE: ....

> **1.** **To Set up a Simple Electric Circuit To Measure and Show the Relationship Between Current, Voltage and Resistance** *(50.2)*

2. *Planning the Activity:*

   (a) The current in a circuit is measured using an instrument called an .... , which is wired in .... in a circuit. Current is measured in units called ....

   (b) The voltage in a circuit is measured using an instrument called a .... , which is wired in .... in a circuit. Voltage is measured in units called ....

   (c) The resistance in a circuit can be found by dividing the .... by the .... for any given set of values for these. It can also be measured directly using an ....

   (d) If the voltage in the circuit was increased, what effect would this have on the size of the current?

   ....

   (e) The size of the resistance in the heating element depends on the size, shape and the material of which the heating element is made. Provided it does not get too hot, would you expect the resistance to change in size during the experiment? Explain.

   ....

3. *Materials Used:* ....

   ....

   ....

Diagram

*4. **Method:*** ....
....
....
....
....
....
....
....

*5. **Results:*** *Complete the table below to show the corresponding voltages and currents measured:*

Voltage (V)	0							
Current (A)	0							

Draw a graph of Voltage against Current (Voltage on the vertical axis) :

*6. **Conclusions:***

Comment on the shape of the Voltage / Current graph: ....

What is the relationship between voltage and current? ....

Divide each voltage by its corresponding current. What do you notice about the results? ....

....

Voltage divided by current (from Ohm's Law) gives a constant value which is the ....

ACTIVITY REPORT   **Extra Experiment**   DATE: ....

(These pages may be photocopied)

1. *Title:*

2. *Planning the Activity:*

   ....
   ....
   ....
   ....
   ....
   ....

3. *Materials and Apparatus Used:* ....

   ....
   ....
   ....
   ....
   ....

4. *Method:*

   Diagram

5. *Results:*

6. *Conclusions:*

MANDATORY INVESTIGATIONS: LINE-DIAGRAMS FOR WRITE-UPS

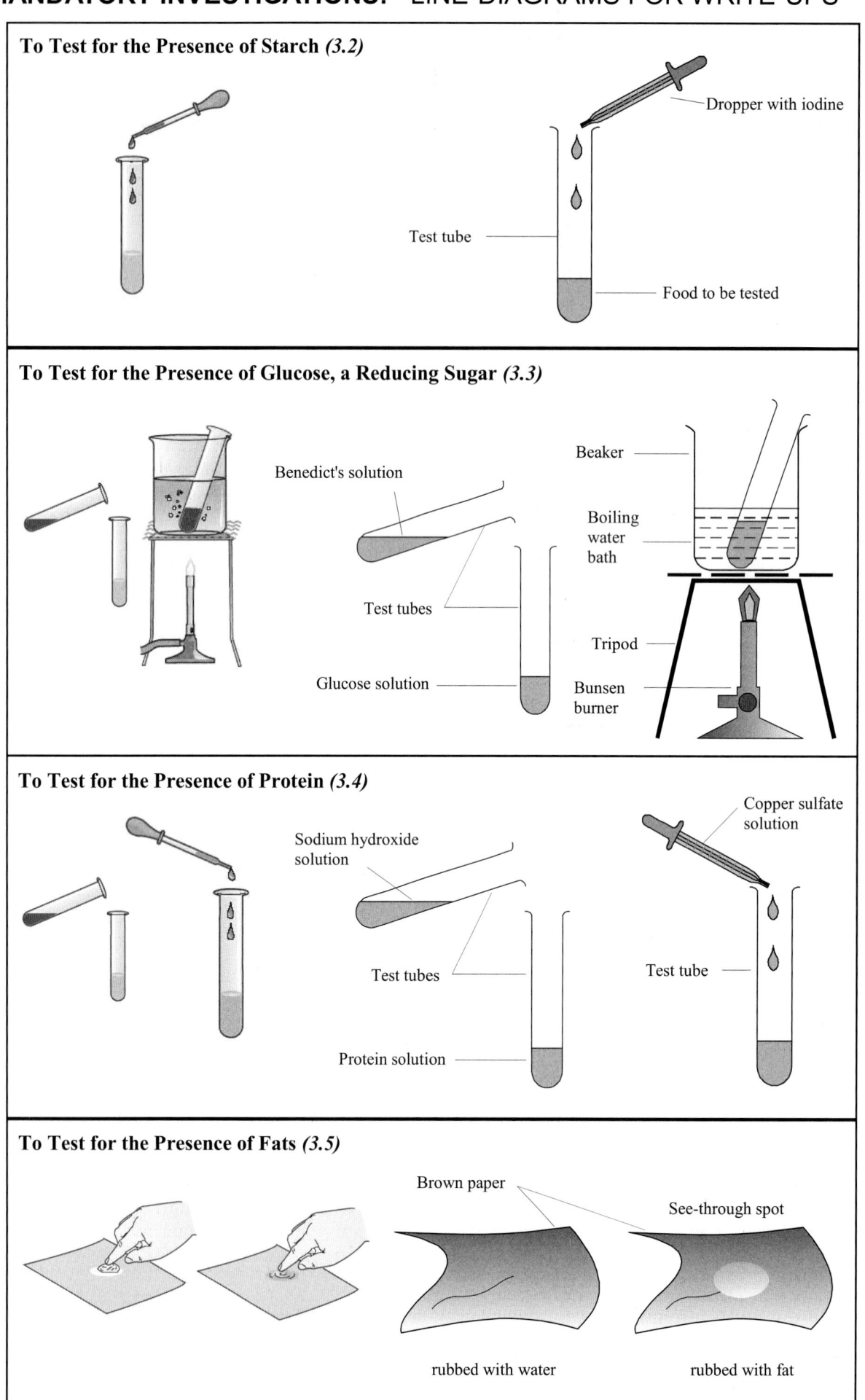

To Test for the Presence of Starch (3.2)

- Dropper with iodine
- Test tube
- Food to be tested

To Test for the Presence of Glucose, a Reducing Sugar (3.3)

- Benedict's solution
- Test tubes
- Glucose solution
- Beaker
- Boiling water bath
- Tripod
- Bunsen burner

To Test for the Presence of Protein (3.4)

- Sodium hydroxide solution
- Test tubes
- Protein solution
- Copper sulfate solution
- Test tube

To Test for the Presence of Fats (3.5)

- Brown paper
- See-through spot
- rubbed with water
- rubbed with fat

To Investigate the Conversion of Chemical Energy in Food to Heat Energy *(3.6)*

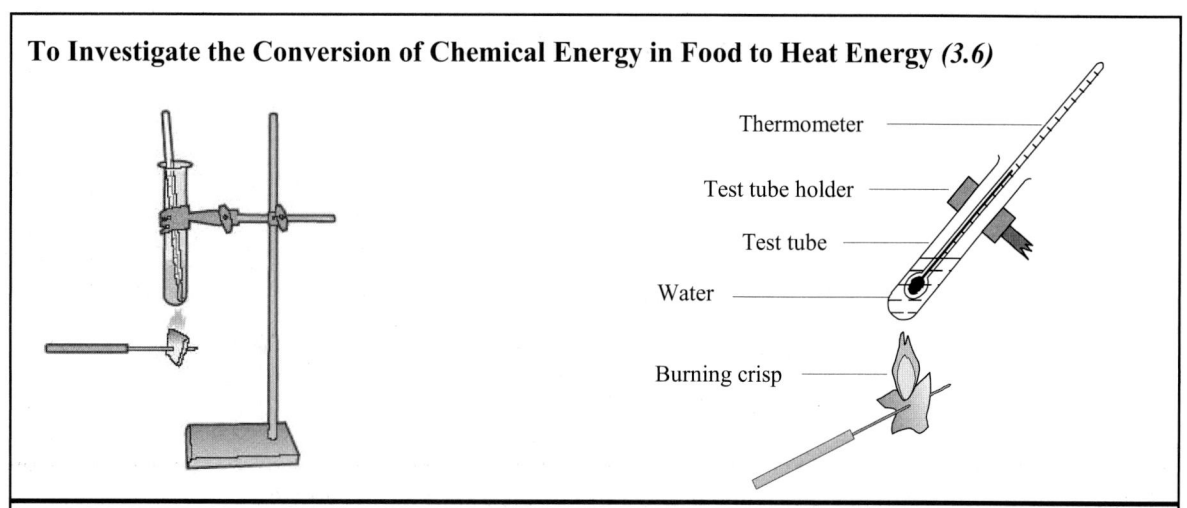

To Show the Action of Amylase on Starch *(4.1)*

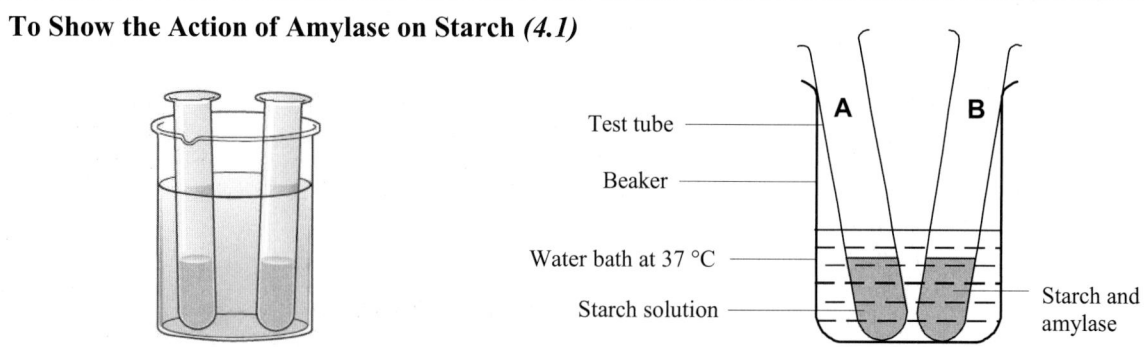

To Show that Expired Air has More Carbon Dioxide than Inspired Air *(5.1)*

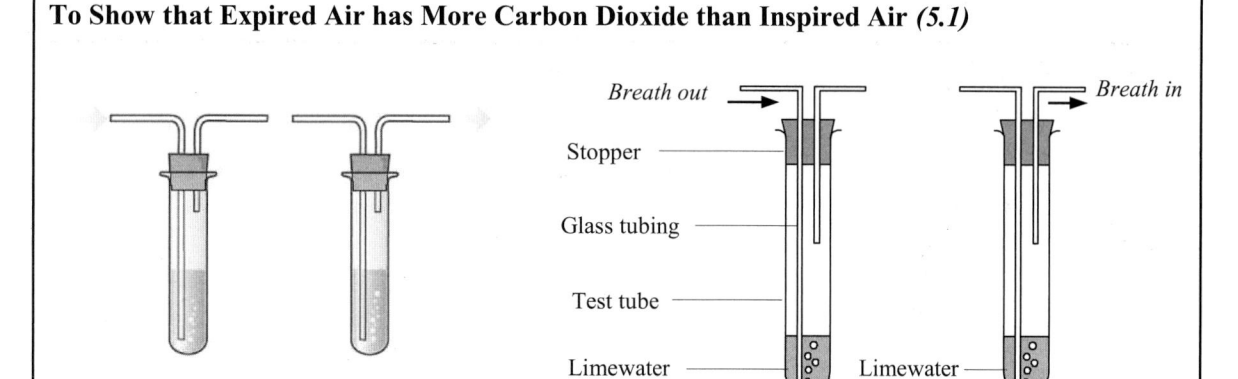

To Show that Starch is Produced in a Photosynthesising Plant *(13.1)*

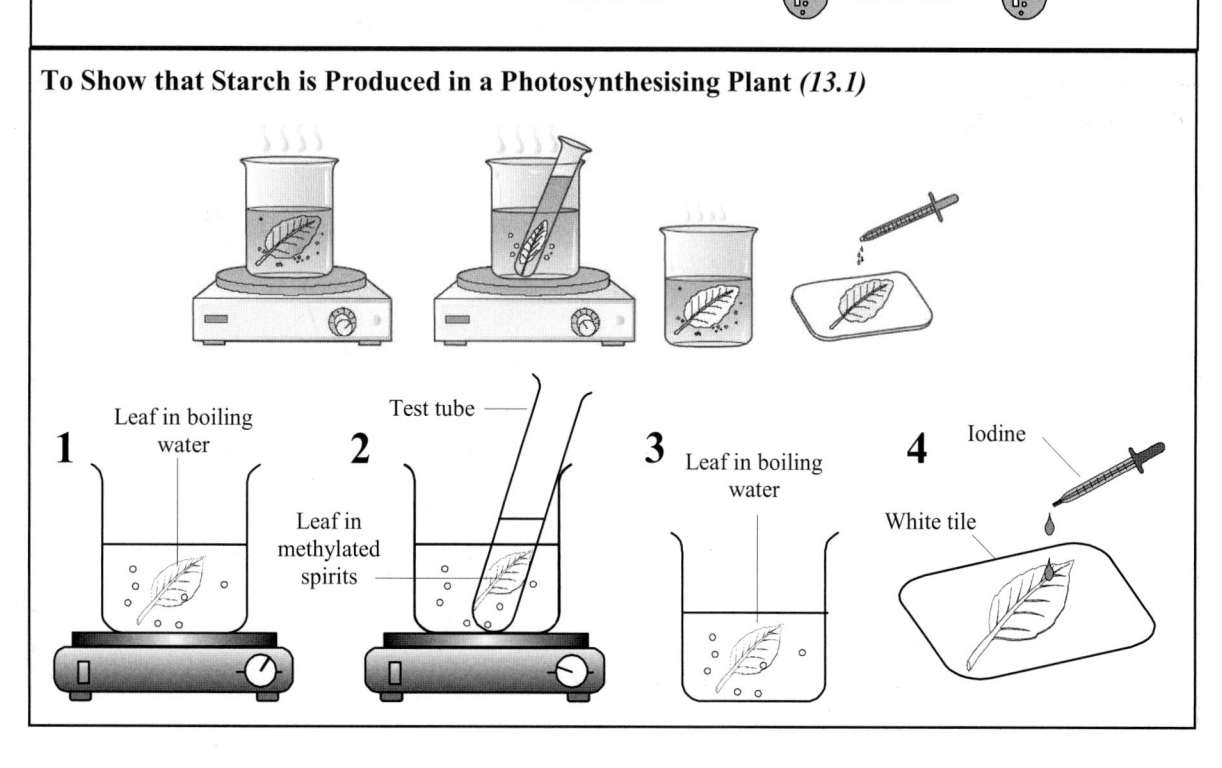

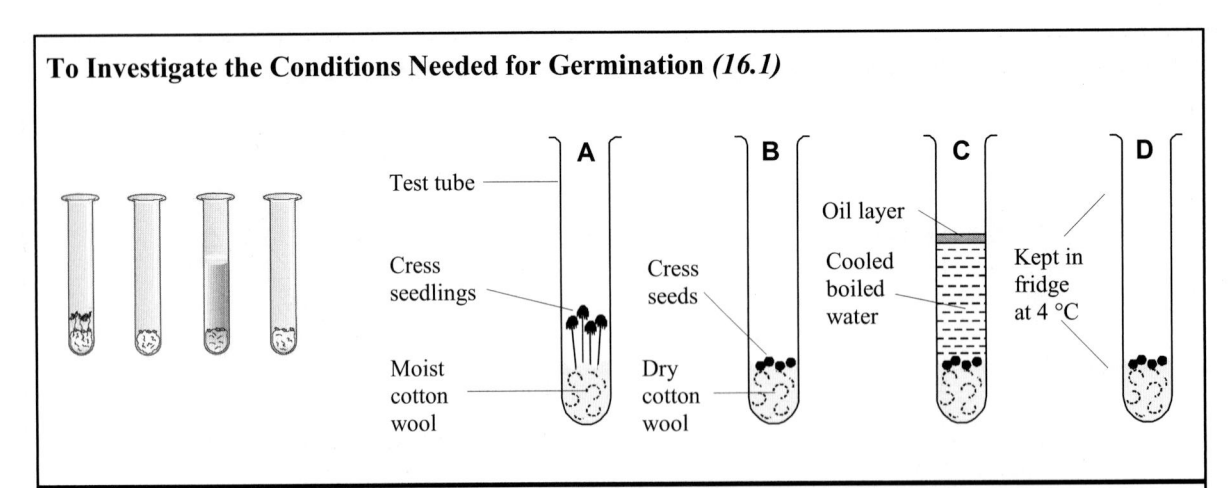

To Investigate the Conditions Needed for Germination *(16.1)*

A — Test tube, Cress seedlings, Moist cotton wool
B — Cress seeds, Dry cotton wool
C — Oil layer, Cooled boiled water
D — Kept in fridge at 4 °C

To Investigate the Presence of Bacteria and Fungi in Air and Soil *(20.1/20.2)*

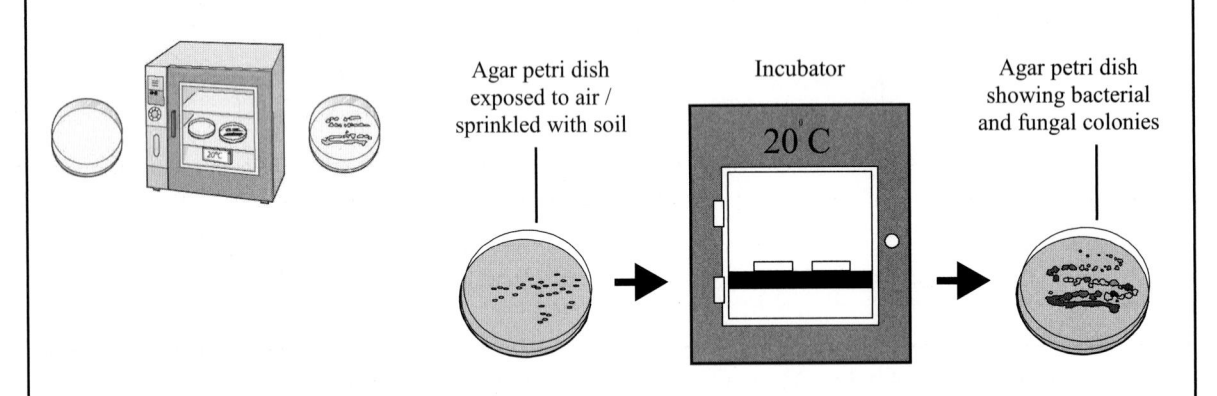

Agar petri dish exposed to air / sprinkled with soil → Incubator 20 °C → Agar petri dish showing bacterial and fungal colonies

To Grow Crystals of Copper Sulfate *(23.3)*

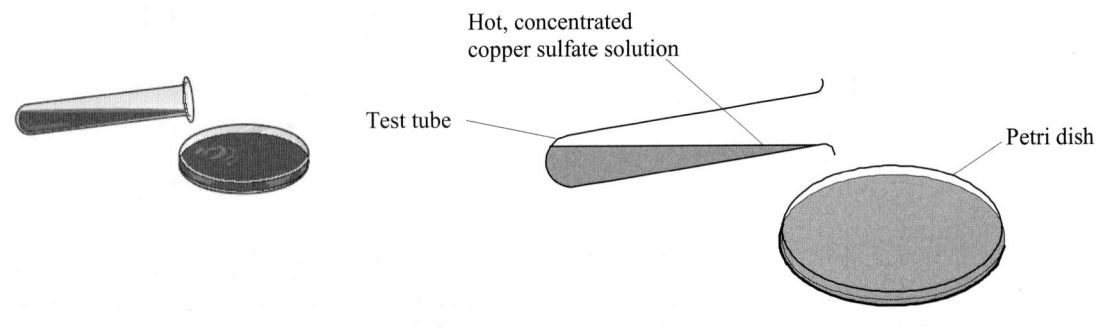

Hot, concentrated copper sulfate solution — Test tube — Petri dish

To Separate Sand and Water by Filtration *(24.1)*

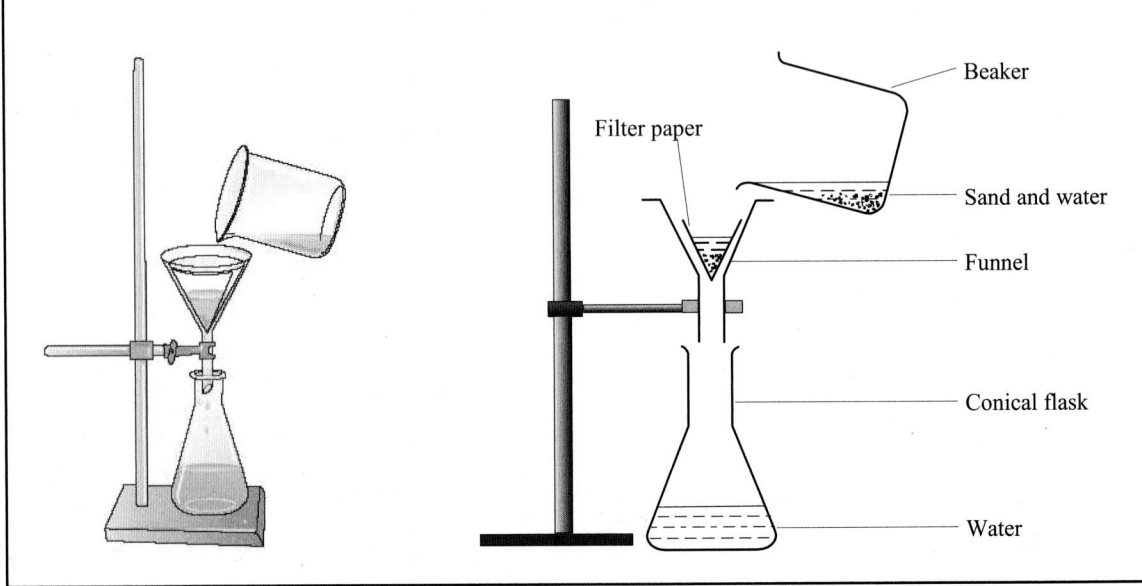

Beaker, Filter paper, Sand and water, Funnel, Conical flask, Water

To Separate Sand, Salt and Water by Filtration and Evaporation (24.2)

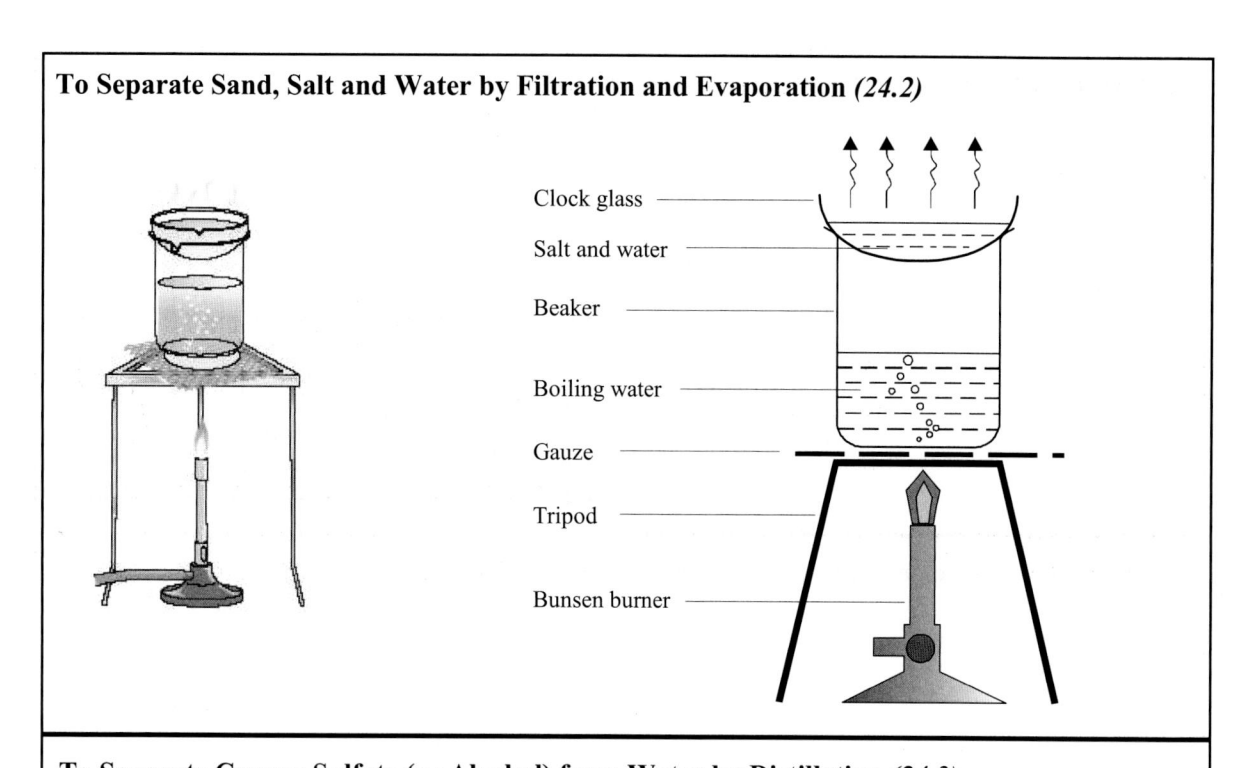

- Clock glass
- Salt and water
- Beaker
- Boiling water
- Gauze
- Tripod
- Bunsen burner

To Separate Copper Sulfate (or Alcohol) from Water by Distillation (24.3)

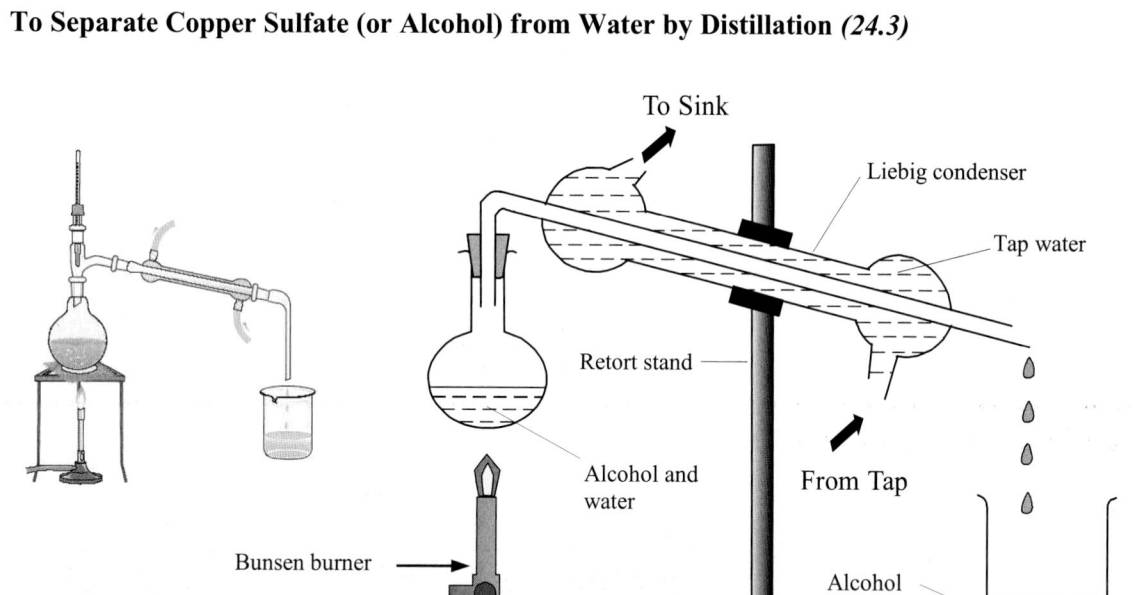

- To Sink
- Liebig condenser
- Tap water
- Retort stand
- Alcohol and water
- From Tap
- Bunsen burner
- Alcohol

To Separate the Dyes in Ink by Paper Chromatography (24.4)

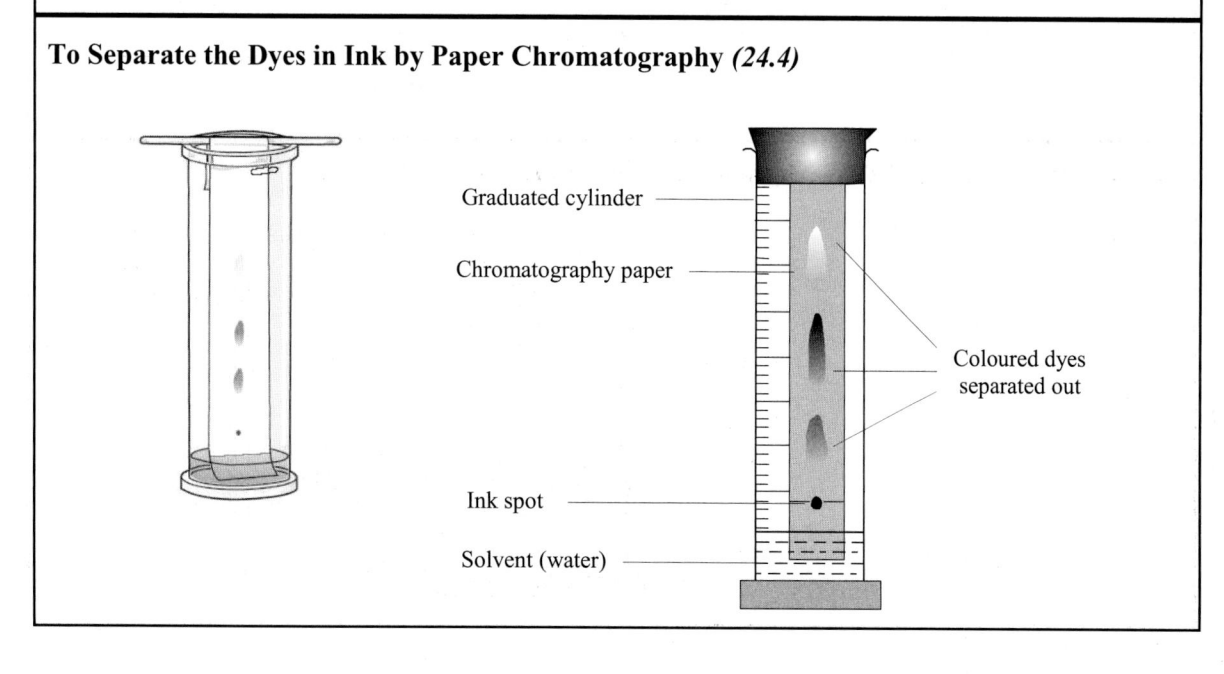

- Graduated cylinder
- Chromatography paper
- Coloured dyes separated out
- Ink spot
- Solvent (water)

To Test the pH of a Variety of Materials using the pH Scale *(30.1)*

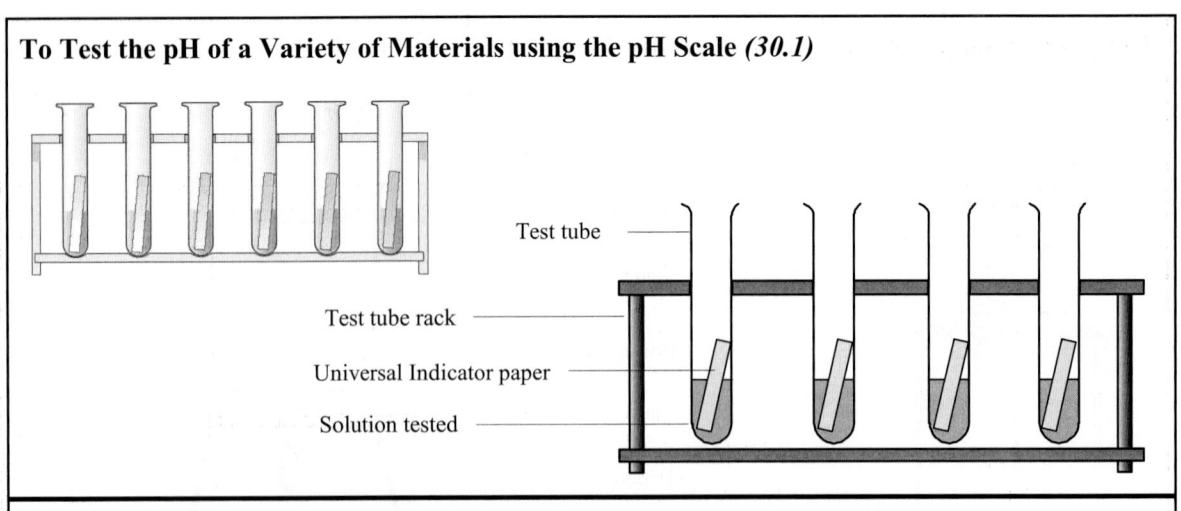

- Test tube
- Test tube rack
- Universal Indicator paper
- Solution tested

To Titrate Hydrochloric Acid (HCl) Against Sodium Hydroxide (NaOH) *(30.3)*

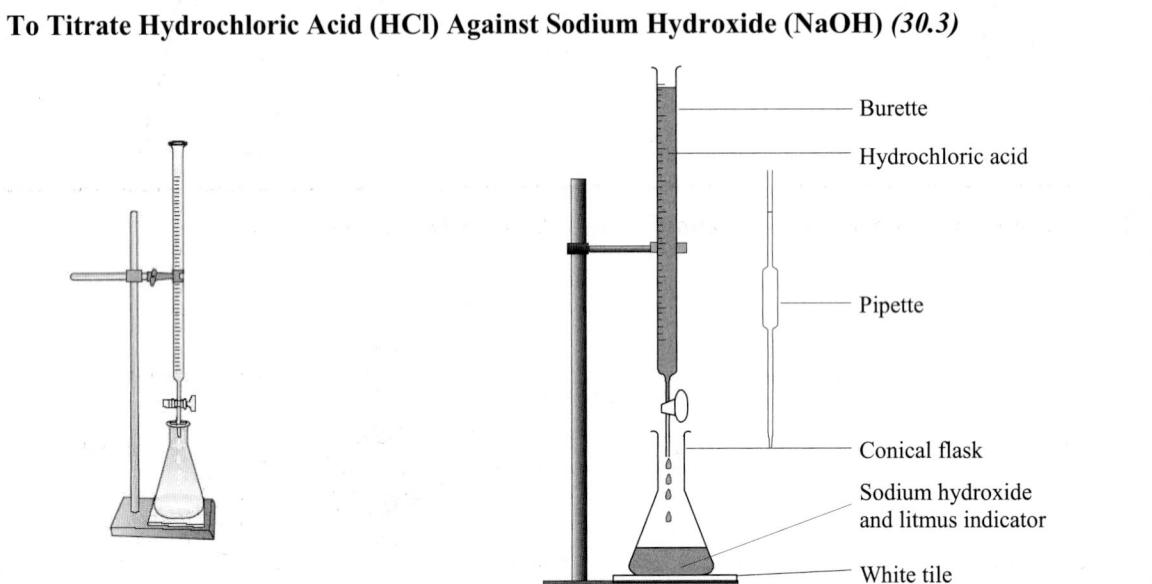

- Burette
- Hydrochloric acid
- Pipette
- Conical flask
- Sodium hydroxide and litmus indicator
- White tile

To Measure the Percentage of Oxygen in Air *(31.1)*

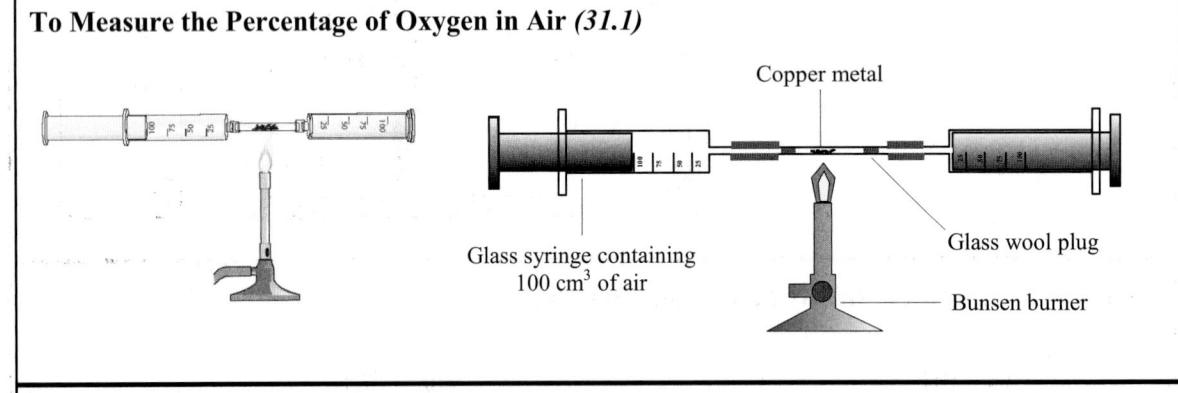

- Copper metal
- Glass syringe containing 100 cm^3 of air
- Glass wool plug
- Bunsen burner

To Show the Presence of Water Vapour and Carbon Dioxide in Air *(31.2)*

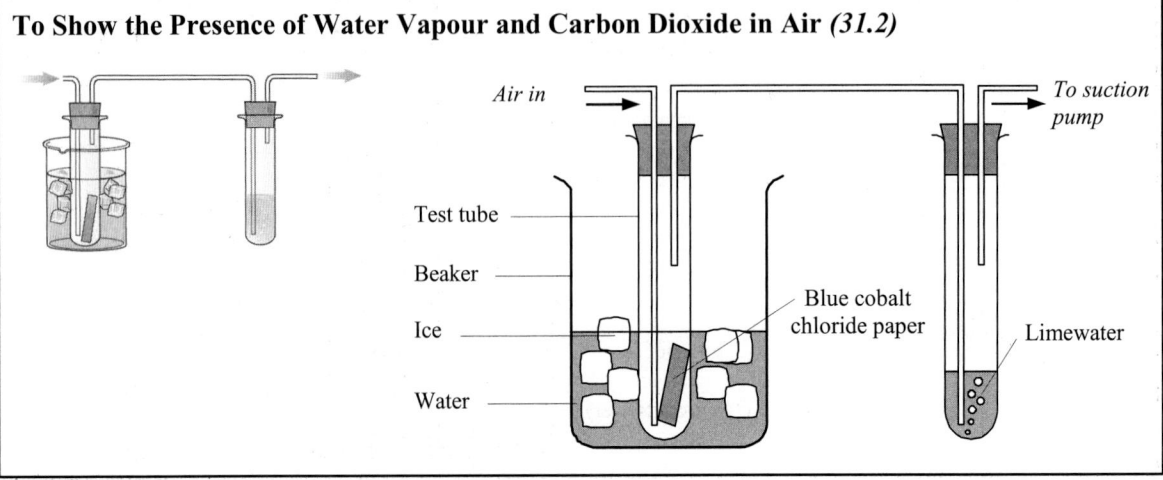

- Air in
- To suction pump
- Test tube
- Beaker
- Ice
- Water
- Blue cobalt chloride paper
- Limewater

To Prepare Oxygen Gas *(31.3)*

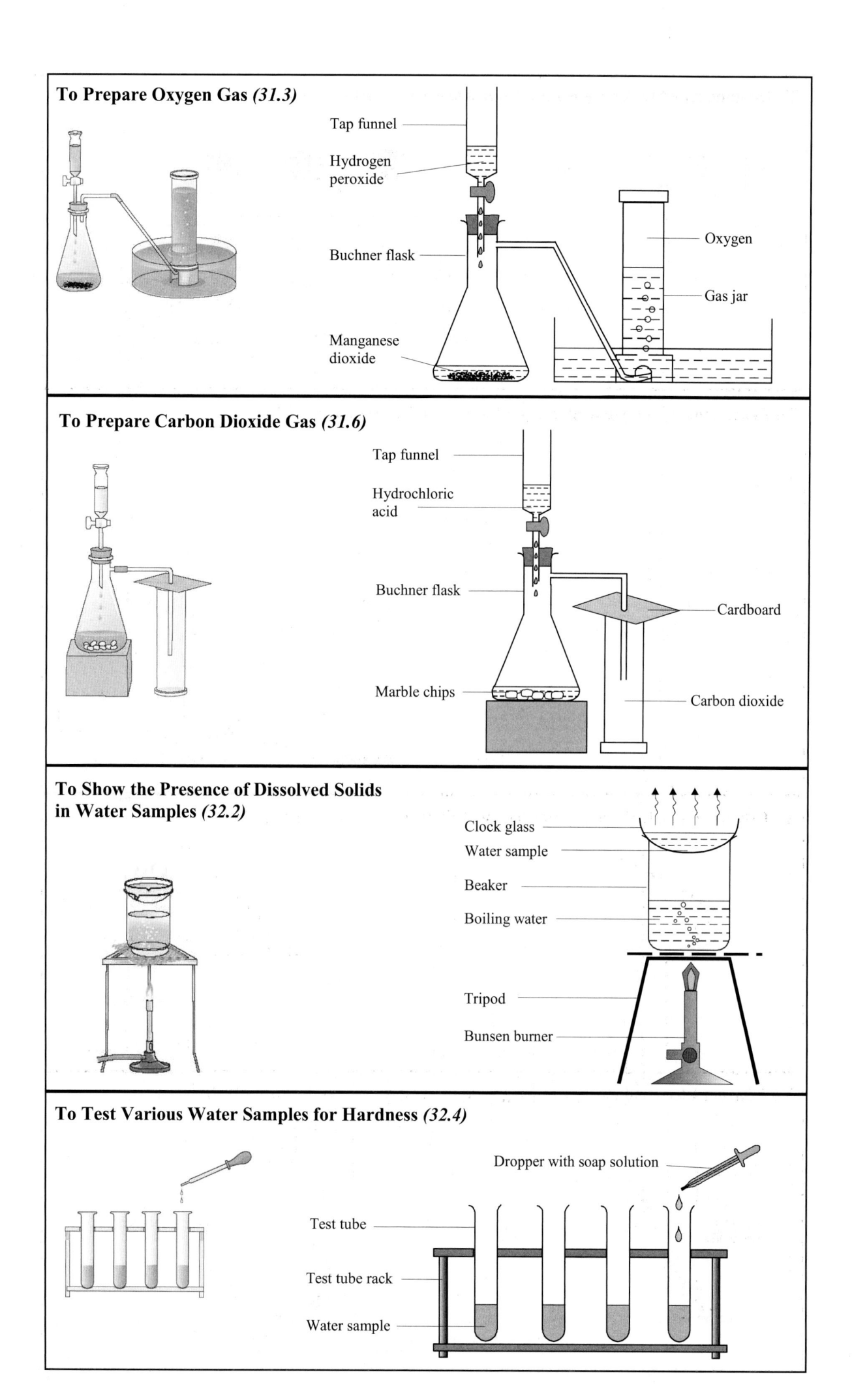

- Tap funnel
- Hydrogen peroxide
- Buchner flask
- Manganese dioxide
- Oxygen
- Gas jar

To Prepare Carbon Dioxide Gas *(31.6)*

- Tap funnel
- Hydrochloric acid
- Buchner flask
- Marble chips
- Cardboard
- Carbon dioxide

To Show the Presence of Dissolved Solids in Water Samples *(32.2)*

- Clock glass
- Water sample
- Beaker
- Boiling water
- Tripod
- Bunsen burner

To Test Various Water Samples for Hardness *(32.4)*

- Dropper with soap solution
- Test tube
- Test tube rack
- Water sample

To Demonstrate that Oxygen and Water are Necessary for Rusting *(34.1)*

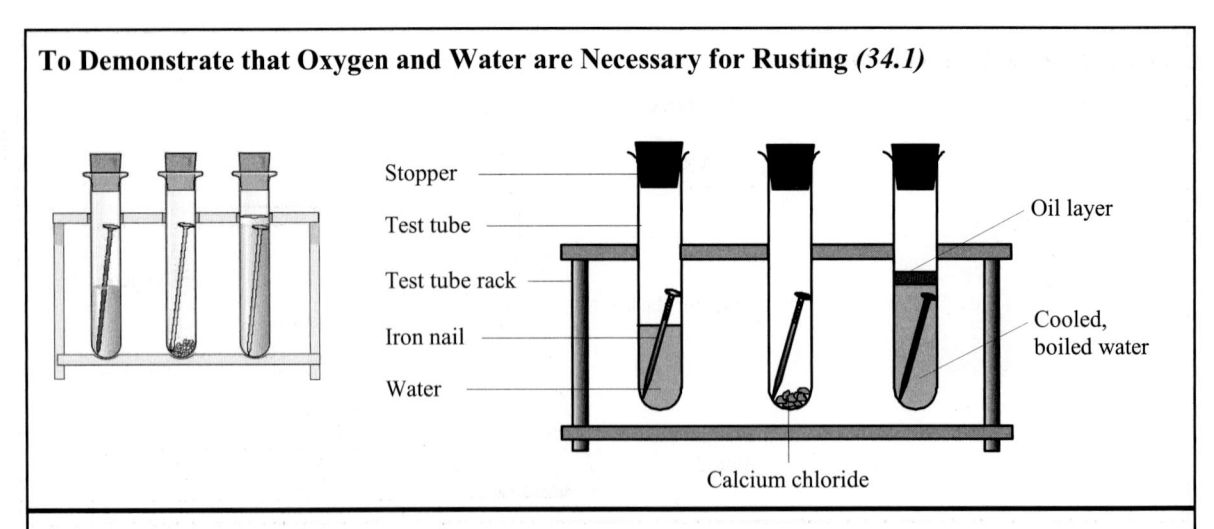

- Stopper
- Test tube
- Test tube rack
- Iron nail
- Water
- Oil layer
- Cooled, boiled water
- Calcium chloride

To React Zinc with Hydrochloric Acid and Test for Hydrogen *(34.3)*

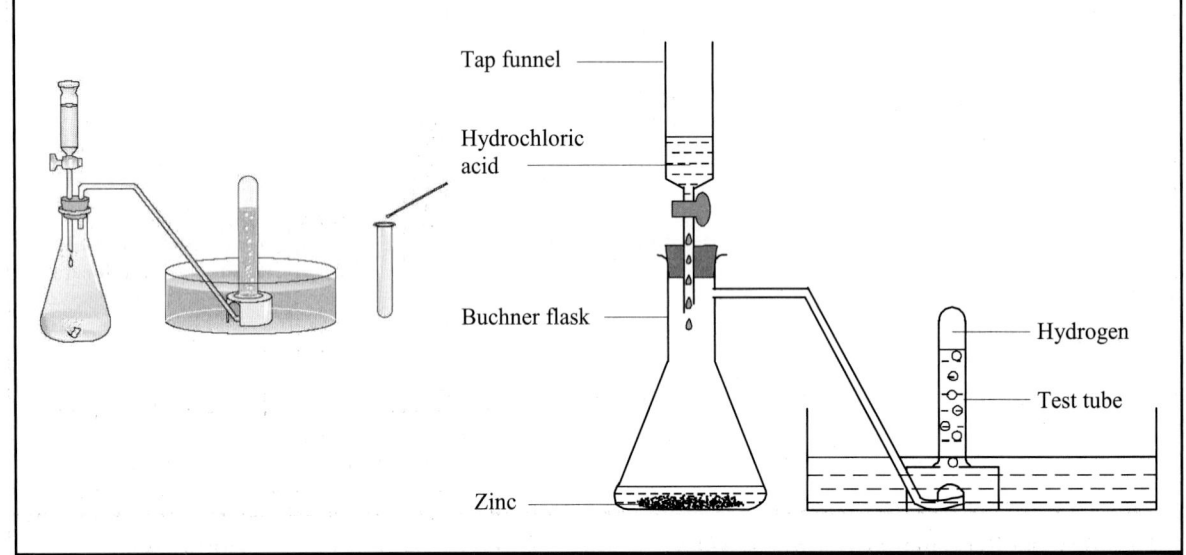

- Tap funnel
- Hydrochloric acid
- Buchner flask
- Zinc
- Hydrogen
- Test tube

To Convert Chemical Energy to Electrical Energy to Heat Energy *(37.2)*

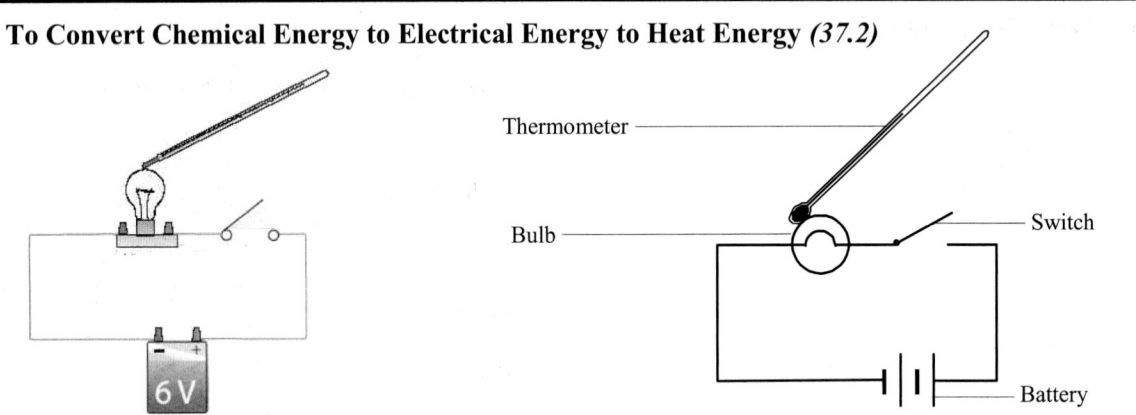

- Thermometer
- Bulb
- Switch
- Battery

To Convert Electrical Energy to Magnetic Energy to Kinetic Energy *(37.3)*

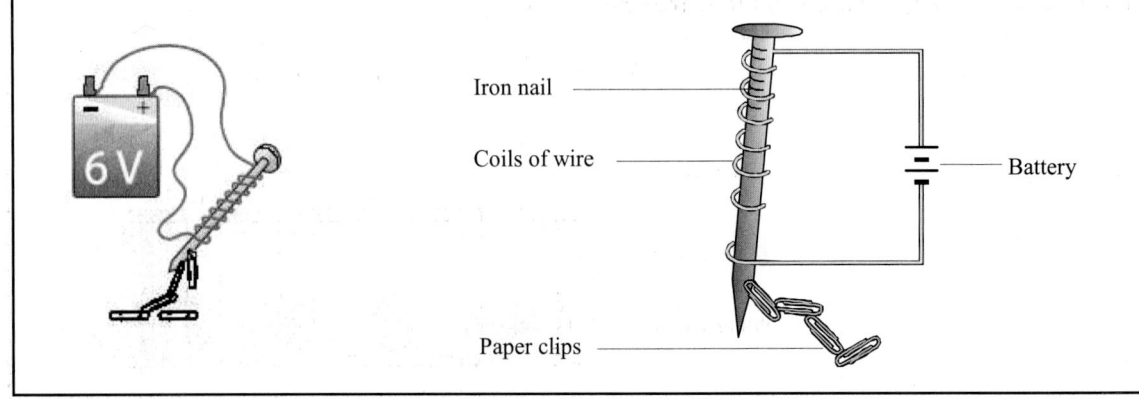

- Iron nail
- Coils of wire
- Battery
- Paper clips

To Convert Light Energy to Electrical Energy to Kinetic Energy *(37.4)*

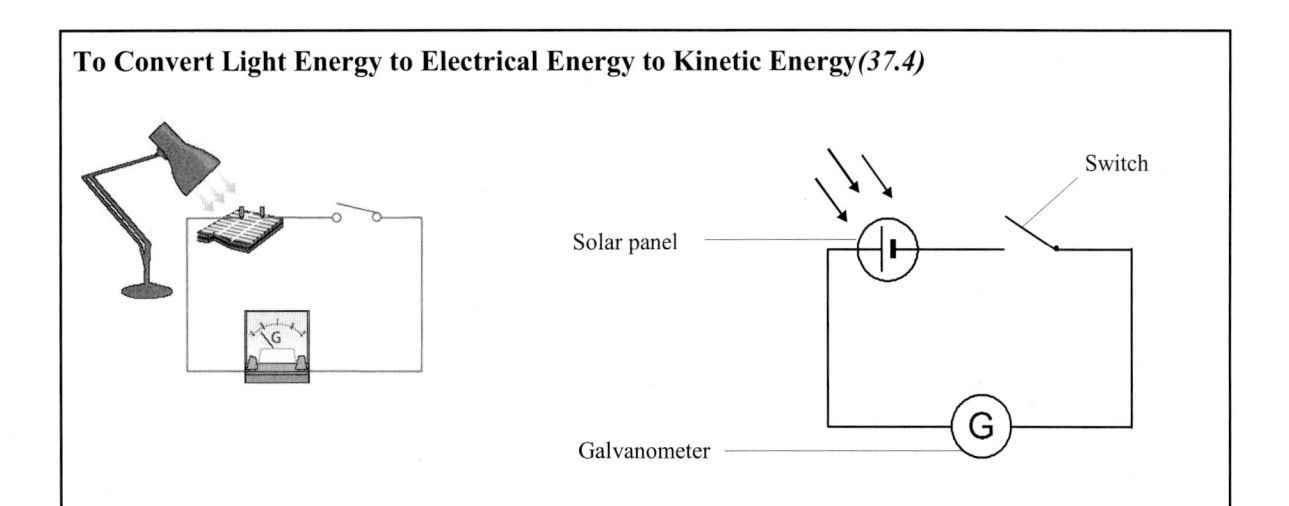

Solar panel
Switch
Galvanometer

To Find the Density of a Regularly-Shaped Solid (e.g. A Block of Wood) *(39.1)*

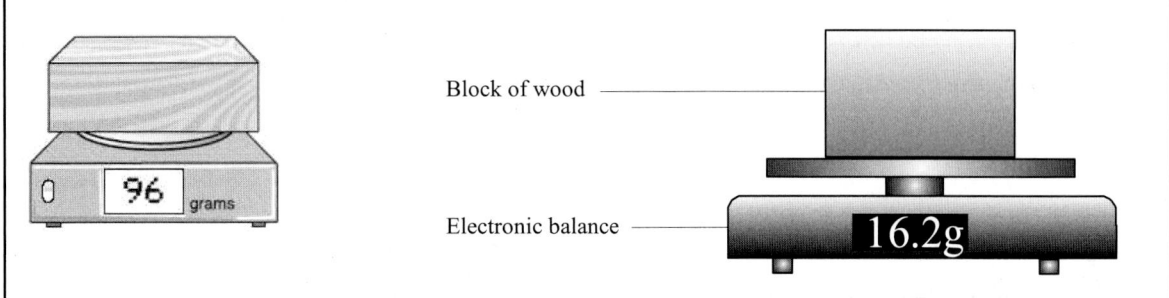

96 grams
Block of wood
Electronic balance
16.2g

To Find the Density of an Irregularly-Shaped Solid (e.g. a stone) *(39.2)*

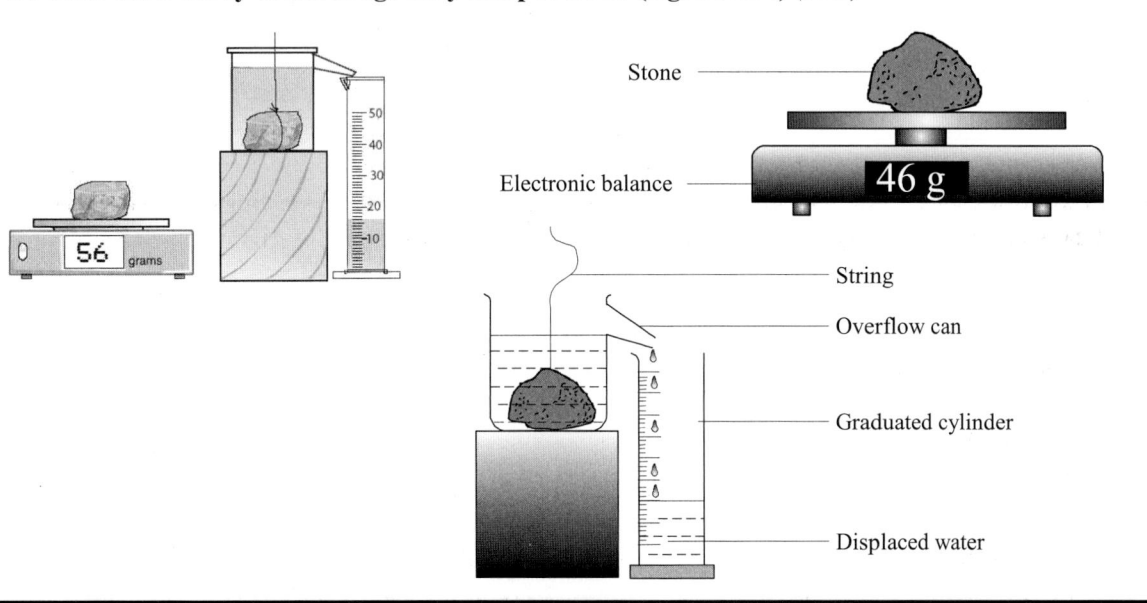

56 grams
Stone
Electronic balance
46 g
String
Overflow can
Graduated cylinder
Displaced water

To Find the Density of a Liquid (e.g. Water and Methylated Spirits) *(39.3)*

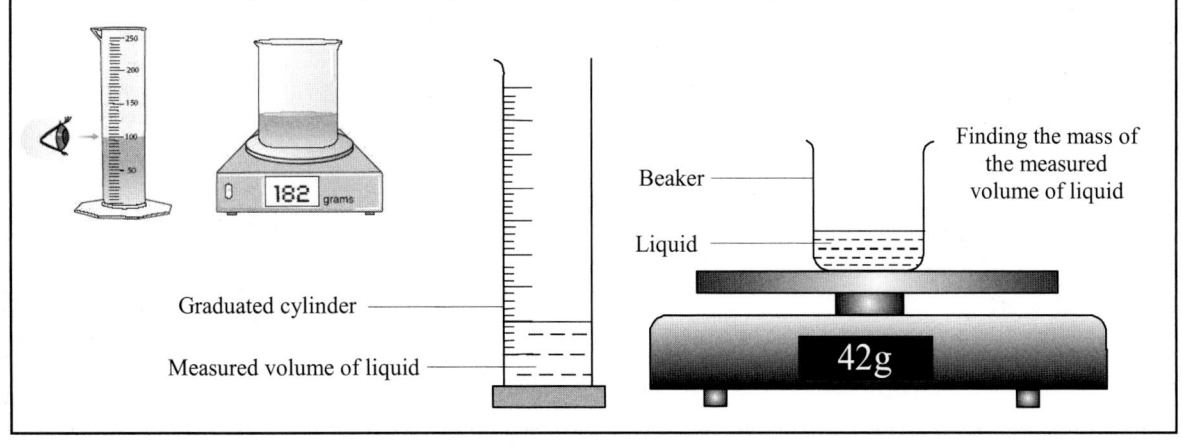

182 grams
Graduated cylinder
Measured volume of liquid
Beaker
Liquid
Finding the mass of the measured volume of liquid
42g

To Investigate the Relationship Between the Extension of a Stretched Spring and the Force Applied to it *(40.1)*

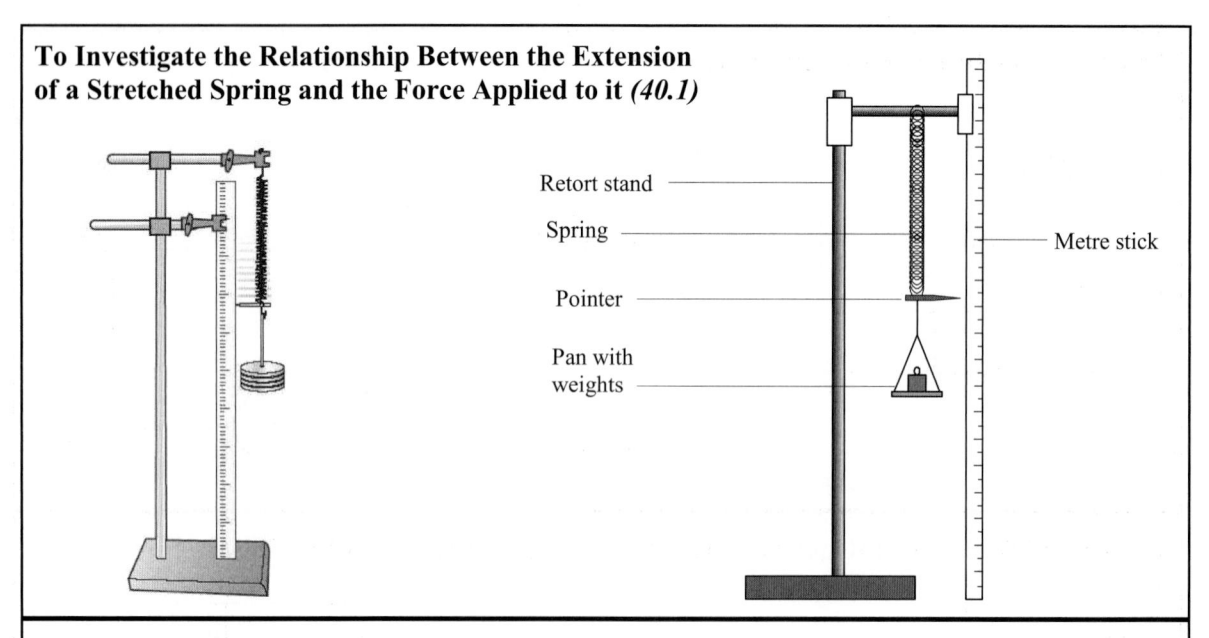

- Retort stand
- Spring
- Pointer
- Pan with weights
- Metre stick

To Compare the Conductivity of Various Metals *(44.1)*

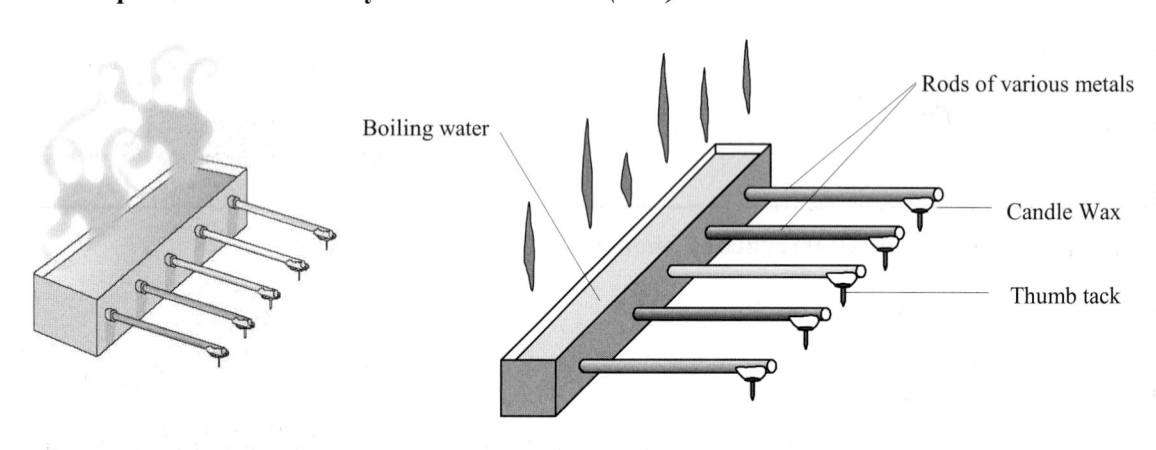

- Boiling water
- Rods of various metals
- Candle Wax
- Thumb tack

To Show that Water is a Poor Conductor of Heat *(44.2)*

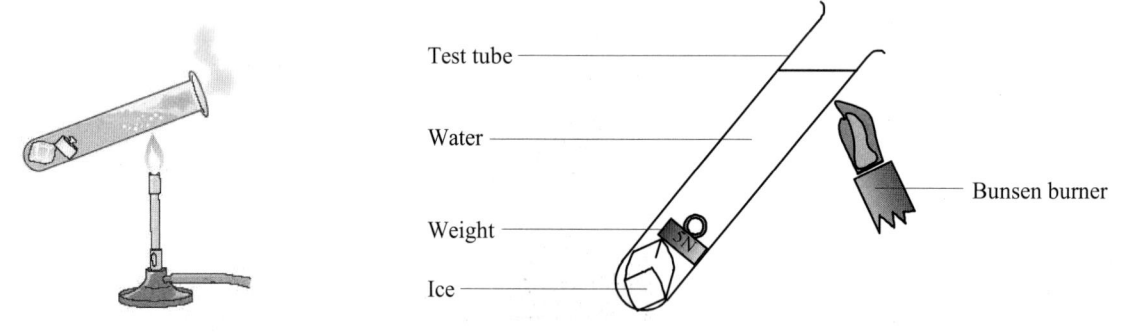

- Test tube
- Water
- Weight
- Ice
- Bunsen burner

To Show Convection Currents in Water *(44.3)*

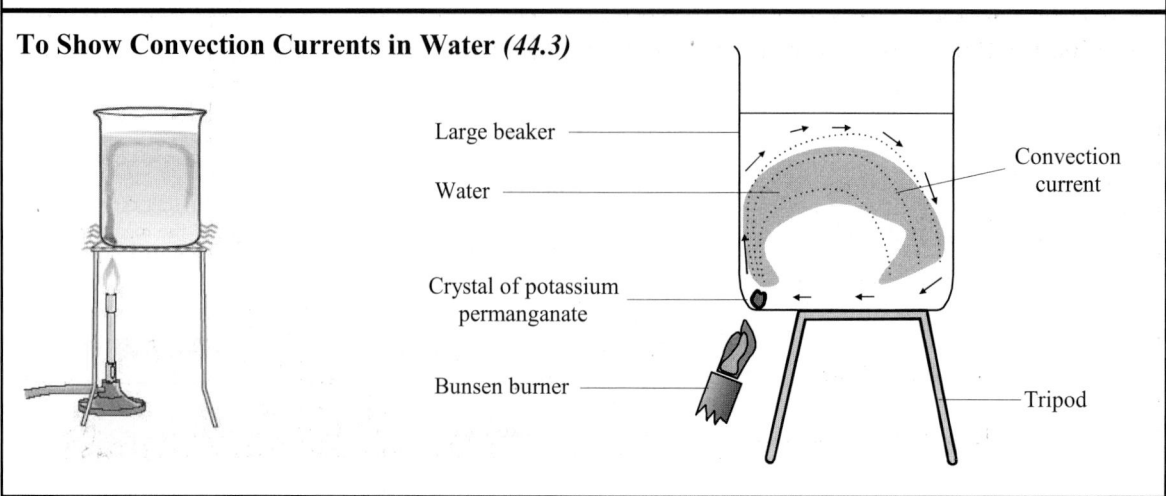

- Large beaker
- Water
- Crystal of potassium permanganate
- Bunsen burner
- Convection current
- Tripod

To Show Heat Transfer by Radiation *(44.4)*

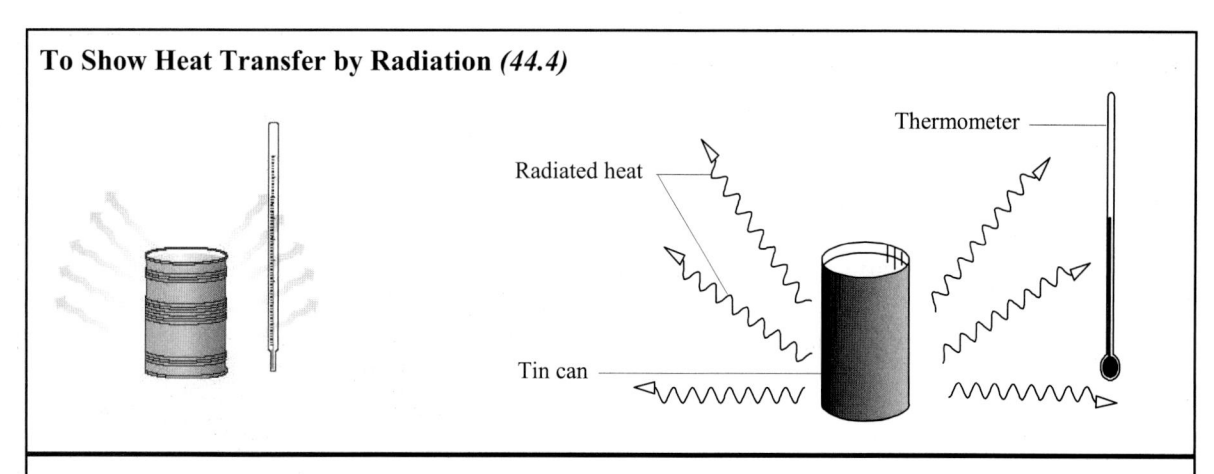

Radiated heat

Thermometer

Tin can

To Show that Solids Expand when Heated and Contract when Cooled *(44.5)*

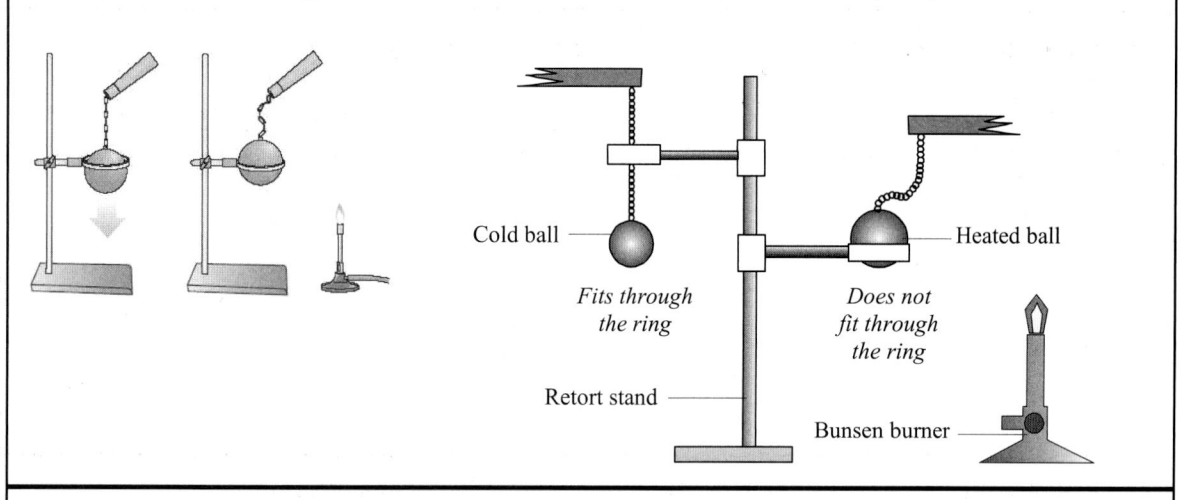

Cold ball — *Fits through the ring*

Heated ball — *Does not fit through the ring*

Retort stand

Bunsen burner

To Show that Liquids Expand when Heated and Contract when Cooled *(44.6)*

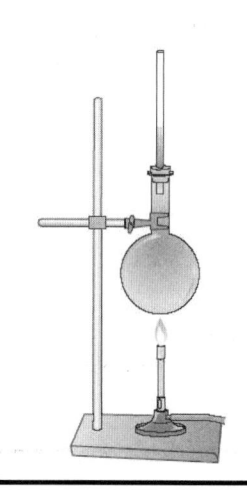

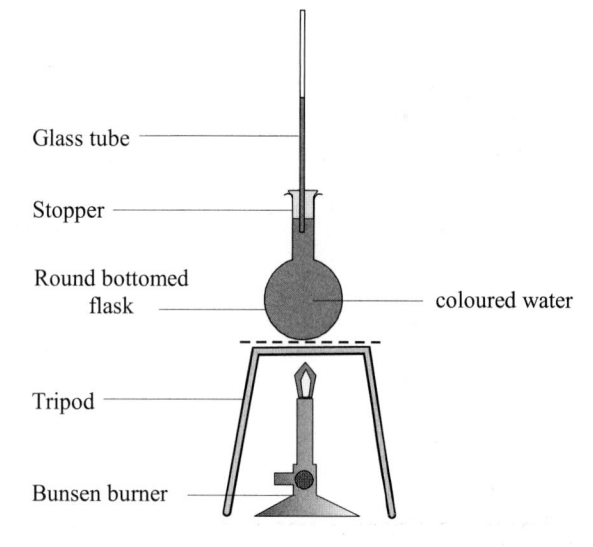

Glass tube

Stopper

Round bottomed flask — coloured water

Tripod

Bunsen burner

To Show that Gases Expand when Heated and Contract when Cooled *(44.7)*

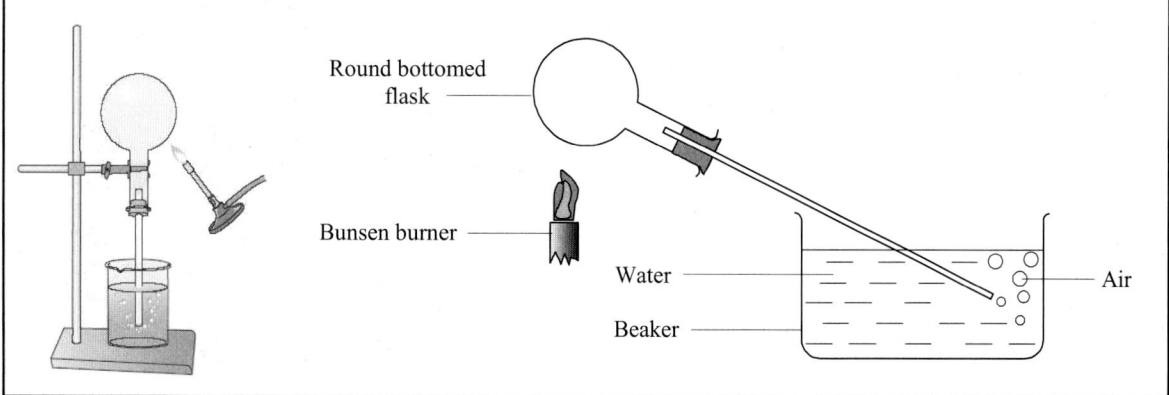

Round bottomed flask

Bunsen burner

Water

Beaker

Air

To Show that Light Travels in Straight Lines *(46.1)*

Lamp

Cardboard square

To Investigate the Reflection of Light by a Plane Mirror *(46.2a)*

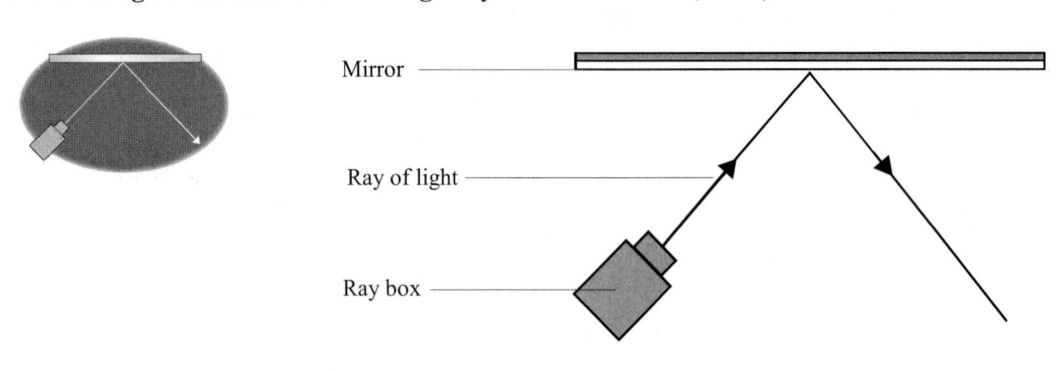

Mirror

Ray of light

Ray box

To Demonstrate and Explain the Operation of a Simple Periscope *(46.2b)*

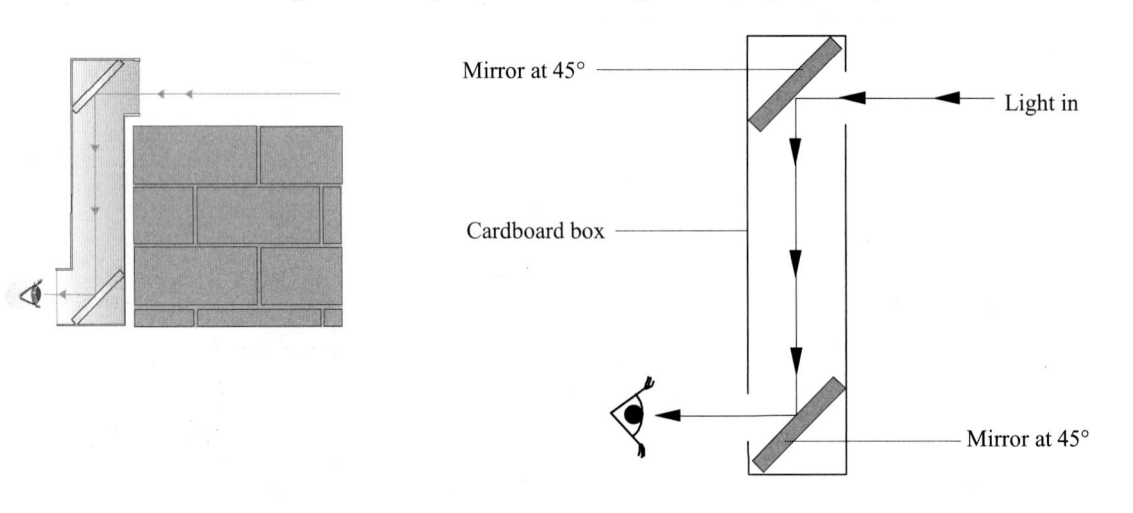

Mirror at 45°

Light in

Cardboard box

Mirror at 45°

To Plot the Magnetic Field of a Bar Magnet *(48.5)*

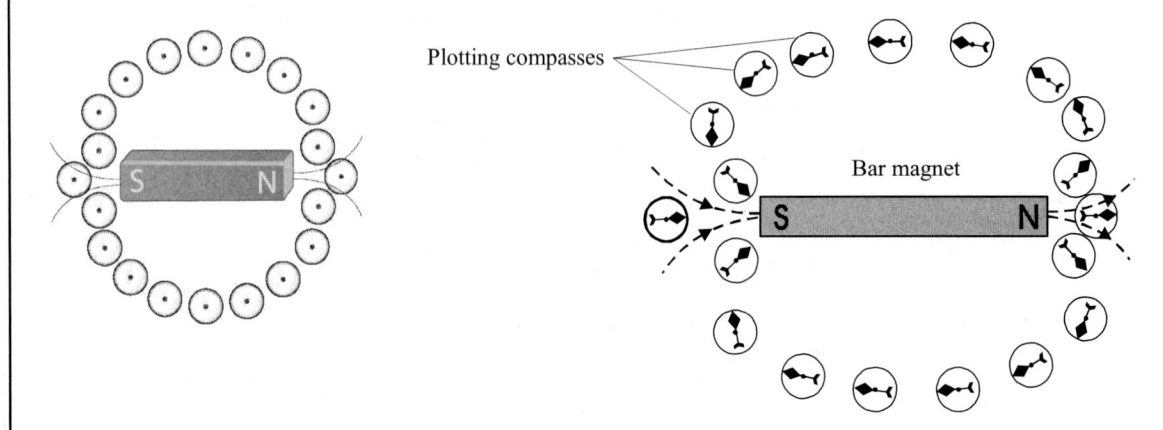

Plotting compasses

Bar magnet

To Distinguish Between Conductors and Insulators *(50.1)*

Battery

Lamp

Conductor/Insulator

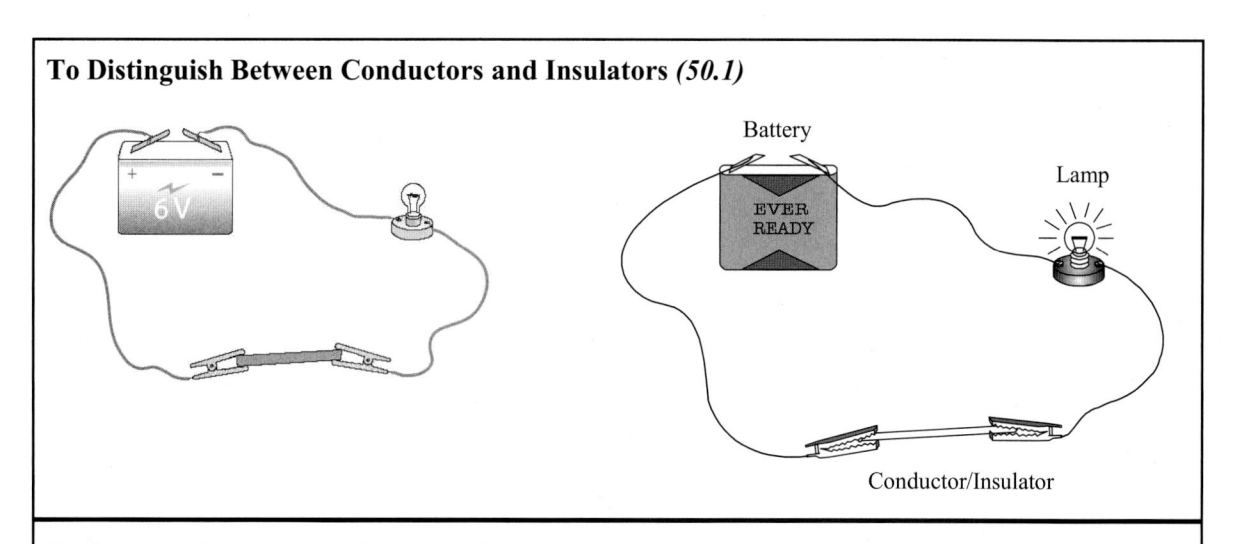

To Set Up a Simple Electrical Circuit and Measure Current, Voltage and Resistance and Show the Relationship Between Them *(50.2)*

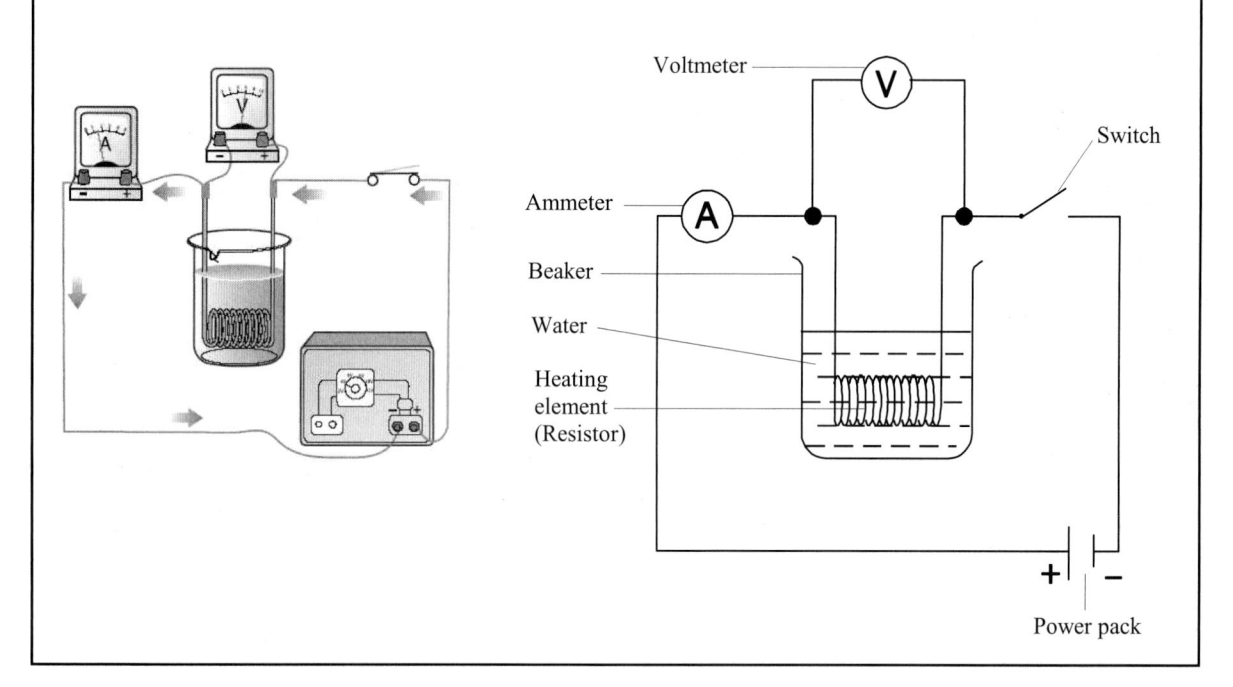

Voltmeter

Switch

Ammeter

Beaker

Water

Heating element (Resistor)

Power pack